I0825080

DEATH IN THE STRIKE ZONE

THE MYSTERY OF AMERICA'S FIRST BASEBALL HERO

THOMAS W. GILBERT

GODINE
BOSTON

Published in 2026 by
GODINE
Boston, Massachusetts
www.godine.com

Copyright 2026 © by Thomas W. Gilbert

All Rights Reserved.
No part of this book may be used or reproduced in any manner whatsoever without written permission from the publisher, except in the case of brief quotations embodied in critical articles and reviews.
For more information, please visit our website.

Text design by Alex Camlin

Library of Congress Cataloging-in-Publication Data

Title: Death in the Strike Zone : The Mystery of America's First Baseball Hero / Thomas W. Gilbert.
Description: Boston, Massachusetts : Godine, 2026.
Identifiers: LCCN 2025042565 (print) | LCCN 2025042566 (ebook)
| ISBN 9781567927597 hardcover | ISBN 9781567927603 epub
Subjects: LCSH: Creighton, James, 1841-1862 | Brooklyn Excelsiors (Baseball team)—History—19th century | Baseball players—United States—Biography | Baseball—United States—History—19th century | Baseball injuries—United States—History—19th century | LCGFT: Biographies
Classification: LCC GV865.C679 G55 2026 (print) | LCC GV865.C679 (ebook)
LC record available at https://lccn.loc.gov/2025042565
LC ebook record available at https://lccn.loc.gov/2025042566

First Printing, 2026
Printed in the United States of America

Also by Thomas W. Gilbert

How Baseball Happened: Outrageous Lies Exposed! The True Story Revealed

CONTENTS

James Creighton's shocking 1862 death inspired America's first baseball-themed monument, which still stands in Brooklyn's Green-Wood Cemetery.

1 JAMES WHO?

I WILL TELL YOU A MYSTERY.

He was the greatest American athlete of his time. He was the first famous baseball player. The first baseball card has his picture on it. He threw the first fastball *and* the first curveball. He is the reason why baseball has a strike zone.

His name was James Creighton. You have probably never heard of him. That is a part of the mystery.

Creighton's career was as bright as a supernova and just as brief. He died in 1862 when he was only 21 years old. Before that, Creighton was the player little boys pretended to be. Never-before-seen crowds turned out to see him. Baseball players made pilgrimages to his grave. Clubs were named after him. He inspired a great novel. Yet, somehow, he is not in the Hall of Fame, and most of what it says about him in baseball histories is wrong. The book you are holding in your hands is his first biography.

The mystery of Creighton is alive and waiting to be solved. It is baseball's oldest and coldest cold case. It is a mystery that contains other mysteries — a whodunit and also a how-done-it. Baseball tends to change gradually — pitchers throw harder; players grow stronger; run totals trend up or down. But James Creighton's pitching revolution arrived with the suddenness of a tsunami. It came out of nowhere, swept away the old way of playing and changed the game in ways that we can feel today.

We know that James Creighton was righthanded. We know that he threw much, much harder than anyone before him, with lethal movement and exquisite control. He almost never lost. But we do not know how he did it. We do not even know what to call the pitches he was throwing. Even batters who faced him were not sure. There are other unanswered questions. Were his pitches legal? How did he die?

Like a detective investigating an unsolved case, to find answers we must blow the metaphorical dust off ancient case files, open them up and look at them with new eyes. Our witnesses are dead, and finding anything new about someone who died 160 years ago would seem to be a longshot. Incredibly, I was able to find new evidence (including what could be baseball's first big gambling scandal). Still, getting to the bottom of the mystery of James Creighton will be like trying to solve a jigsaw puzzle without all the pieces.

There is one thing we will never know: what Creighton was like as a person. We know what he looked like. Judging from a photograph of his last club, the Brooklyn Excelsiors, he was about 5'7" and 150 pounds. Today, he would be one of the smallest players in major-league baseball, but he was close to average for the 1860s. Creighton's obituaries praise him in the maddeningly bland way that you would expect when a great athlete dies young. The one specific they give us is that Creighton was an amateur musician, but this may be nothing more than the Victorian equivalent of saying that a young man of today enjoyed social media or gaming.

The greatest mystery is not that we have forgotten who James Creighton was, but that we have forgotten what he did.

The passage of time is not enough to explain Creighton's predicament. Not all the dead are forgotten. Fundamental to history is the question of who is remembered and why. Babe Ruth retired almost 100 years ago, and even non-baseball fans know who he was. James Creighton changed baseball more than Ruth did. Like Ruth and Shohei Ohtani, Creighton was a two-way player, excelling on both sides of the ball. Unlike those two, he never played in the majors; in fact, he never played a single game of professional baseball. This is because there was no professional baseball. The first professional league was founded nine years after his death. The Baseball Hall of Fame does not admit players from the so-called Amateur Era unless they went on to do something for Major League Baseball, and the blank space on the wall in Cooperstown where his plaque should be partly explains Creighton's obscurity. But the main reason that Creighton has been forgotten is that he has been so colossally misunderstood. This was true even in his own time. People who saw him play—even batters that faced him—could not figure out what he was doing with the baseball.

James Creighton's career is a long list of firsts. He pitched baseball's first shutout. He was not only the best baseball player of his day, but the best American athlete, period. He was such a rare talent that two sports changed their rules for him. When he joined the Brooklyn Stars, a youth club, they immediately began beating the best adult clubs. This has no parallel. There is no major league superstar who, if he were added to, say, a college team, would make it competitive with the New York Yankees. Today, an immense stream of prospects is supplied to pro sports by a vast scouting and development machine whose tentacles reach around the globe. If a 14-year-old pitcher lights up a radar gun in Boise, San Pedro de Macorís or Taipei, someone in organized baseball knows about it. James Creighton was the first youth athlete who was recruited by an American team sport. He was literally the first baseball "phenom."

There were players who were called pitchers before Creighton, but he was the first pitcher in the modern sense of the word, that is, the first to serve as a decisive defensive weapon. When Creighton played, pitchers threw underhand on flat ground. Instead of taking one stride from a pitching rubber, they ran up to a line before delivering a pitch. All fielders played barehanded. Balls could be caught on one bounce for an out. Catchers of this era were the last real men — they stopped pitches and caught foul tips with no gloves, no facemask, and no shin guards or padding of any kind. James Creighton's catcher, Joe Leggett, had it tougher than most because of Creighton's sheer speed. Two years of catching Creighton left Joe Leggett crippled.

James Creighton threw the first fastball that deserved the name. Creighton, not Hall of Famer Candy Cummings, threw the first curveball. Some of Creighton's contemporaries assumed that he was cheating because he was so unhittable, but he wasn't cheating. Baseball

This image of James Creighton appears on what many consider the first baseball card, reproduced and sold to public in the mid-1860s. It is a posed studio shot, but it shows us the start of the twisting, one-stride delivery that enabled Creighton to throw with unheard-of velocity. It may also have killed him.

has exploited and overused too many pitching arms to count, but Creighton was first in this as well. Rumor also had it that Creighton was paid, which would have been another kind of cheating, because in his time baseball was amateur and paying players was against the rules. If true, this is probably another first. Creighton was the everyday pitcher and number-one attraction on the Excelsiors of Brooklyn, a club that was put together to make baseball our first national sport. The Excelsiors took the game from its birthplace, the New York City metropolitan area, by railroad, canal and steamship to upstate New York and America's other big cities: Philadelphia, Baltimore, and Boston. Baseball's first-ever road trips, these expeditions showed the rest of the nation how exciting baseball could be when played by superior athletes. The Excelsiors' tours led straight to the founding of the first national baseball leagues, which became the model for almost every professional sports league in the world.

Even this litany of firsts sells him short. If we want to understand baseball and how it became the National Pastime, we will need to start with solving the mystery of James Creighton.

DEATH DAY

NOBODY IS SUPPOSED TO DIE from playing baseball. Especially not amateur baseball—and certainly not in a meaningless game with nothing at stake at the end of a season that nobody was paying much attention to.

Yet that is how James Creighton, as dominant a pitcher as there has ever been, lost his life in the autumn of 1862.

We have several accounts of James Creighton's death, some from eyewitnesses and some from people who claim to have been eyewitnesses. Comparing them is like watching the classic Kurosawa film *Rashomon*. The more we learn, the less we know.

There was not a lot of serious baseball played in the summer of 1862 in New York and Brooklyn—or anywhere. There had been even less in 1861. The reason was the American Civil War. So many players changed uniforms that most clubs shut down. Ninety or so Excelsiors served in the military. (Amateur Era ballclubs fielded more than one team; they had first nines, second nines and so on). With their large membership they could have kept on going, but it was a bad look to play games while others were fighting and dying at Antietam or Shiloh. Besides, it took a good year and half before Americans stopped expecting that the war would be over in a matter of months. As the shock of the outbreak of war faded, normal life, which in New York included baseball, gradually resumed.

Eighteen-sixty, the last full baseball season before the Civil War, had ended in a crescendo of chaos. James Creighton and his Excelsiors came within one unfinished game of dethroning the perennial champion Atlantics, also of Brooklyn. The whole point of an athletic contest is to produce a winner and a loser, but somehow this one did not. Was it a draw, a forfeit or something else? As far as the Atlantics were concerned, they had successfully defended their title. Most of the baseball community agreed, but not all. In 1862 some sportswriters pointedly called the Excelsiors the champions.

To have two Brooklyn clubs playing for the championship was not the unusual part. Before the Civil War baseball belonged not to the nation but to Brooklyn and New York City, the then-independent cities where the sport was born and raised. In the early 1860s baseball was maturing as a sport, but it still had a long way to go before it could be called the national pastime. There were thousands of clubs, adult and junior, but there were no leagues, schedules or playoffs. Baseball was amateur, which meant that it was against the rules for clubs to compensate their players. Unpacking what the rule makers meant by the word *compensate* would not be a simple task, but the underlying idea was that playing baseball was supposed to be recreation, not a business or a profession. Nearly all amateur ballplayers supported themselves with ordinary jobs. Clubs were true clubs. They were self-constituted and self-governing, and until the end of the Amateur Era they were still social organizations. They played mostly among their own members and faced other clubs only now and then. Championship criteria was another weak area. Somewhat like professional boxing today, baseball championship matches were negotiated by the reigning champion and a challenger. In baseball, whoever beat the old champion (best two out of three) became the new champion.

No championship was at stake on the sunny afternoon of October 14, 1862. Three months earlier the Union Club, which played in then-suburban Morrisania, had beaten the Excelsiors at home. On this day they were traveling to Red Hook, Brooklyn, to play the second game of the series. For most of the past century and a half Red Hook has been a place that seems gray even when the sun is shining—a cheerless zone of warehouses, factories, docks and shipyards. In 1862, however, Red Hook lay outside the developed parts of Brooklyn; it was mostly salt marshes and open fields, barely above sea level. (That has not changed; in 2012 Hurricane Sandy put Red Hook under six feet of water). The Excelsiors relocated there in 1859 because their playing grounds near Carroll Park, created after Bergen Hill was leveled by Irishmen with shovels in the 1840s, were being encroached upon by blocks of new rowhouses. Red Hook was not yet the breeding ground of Italian American mobsters like Al Capone and Frankie Yale, or African American gangs like the El Kovans—in 1935 Brooklyn resident and novelist Thomas Wolfe called Red Hook "a good place to stay away from"—but it had an edge. The *Brooklyn Times-Union* reported in 1862 that Bridget Conway, "a rough, coarse Irish woman," stabbed Joanna Ryan severely in the face and forearm in an argument over whose turn it was to graze their cattle on the Excelsiors' outfield.

It took the Excelsior players twenty minutes to walk, drive a carriage or ride to the game in a horsedrawn streetcar. For the Unions who were coming directly from work in Manhattan, it was a longer trip. There were no subways, and the Brooklyn Bridge had not been built; getting to Brooklyn from Manhattan meant taking one of the many point-to-point ferries that crossed the East River. Those coming all the way from Morrisania took a 30-minute trip on the New York and Harlem Railroad to a station near New York's City Hall Park; then a 20-minute walk to Whitehall Street; across the East River on the Hamilton Ferry; then a ride on the Hamilton Avenue streetcar line to the Court Street stop; finally, another short walk to the foot of Court Street, which ran north-south and ended at the shoreline near where Gowanus Bay opened into Upper New York Bay.

On the east or Gowanus side of lower Court Street stood the Brooklyn Yacht Club and other boating clubs. The Excelsiors played on the west side of the street. To imagine that their grounds looked anything like a modern ballpark would be a mistake. There was a large open field containing baseball diamonds and a freestanding clubhouse, all bounded (at least in part) by a split rail fence. No admission was charged, so fencing that would keep human beings out was not needed. There was a modest sheltered stand near the main infield for female spectators; men and boys stood along the baselines or perched on carriages parked beyond the outfield. The Excelsiors and other top clubs drew spectators, but not many by today's standards. Two years earlier, game one of the 1860 championship series in Red Hook was so packed that there were fans watching from the roof of the yacht club. But foul territory easily accommodated the modest crowd that came on this day in 1862.

It was October, but it was only the Excelsiors' third or fourth game of the season against another club. In late June they had squeaked by the Charter Oak Club by the score of 20–19. Creighton pitched in that game, but he was not his usual unhittable self. The reason was that catcher Joe Leggett's unprotected hands took such a beating that Creighton had to let up on his velocity. The first game of the Union series was played at Morrisania on July 26. In that game the Excelsiors were trailing the Unions, 12–4, when the skies opened up and rain stopped play in the middle of the seventh inning. Creighton was taken out in the fourth inning. This was unusual for an era where pitchers were everyday players and relief pitching as we know it did not exist. It was even more unusual for James Creighton; it was his first pitching loss in two years. And in his career Creighton had been replaced as a pitcher in the middle of a game exactly once before.

The first pitch on October 14th was scheduled for 2:30, but some of the Unions were late and the visitors started the game with eight players. The Excelsiors decided to bat first; in those days the home team had its choice. Durrell, the Unions' ninth man, showed up in the fourth inning. Rarely used backup pitcher Asa Brainard pitched for the Excelsiors and Creighton started the game at second base, which was curious. Bernie Hannegan was pitching for the Unions, which was not. After watching Creighton utterly dominate opposing hitters during the 1860 season, the Unions had gone in search of a pitcher with speed. They did not have to look far. The 17-year-old Hannegan was living with his widowed mother in Morrisania, next door to Union Club founder William Cauldwell. Hannegan started the October 14th game, but, just as curiously, he switched places with the shortstop after one inning. The Excelsiors built a 12–4 lead going into the bottom of the fifth, but Brainard weakened, allowing four runs to shrink the lead to 12–8. At that point another curious thing happened. Creighton came on to pitch in relief, something he almost never did. He stopped the Unions' comeback. After six the score was Excelsiors 13, Unions 9.

The national sports weekly the *New York Clipper* said that Hannegan was replaced because he was "not in condition for play," but according to Henry Chadwick of the Brooklyn *Daily Eagle* newspaper the "Unions became conscience stricken and placed Hyatt as pitcher." Neither paper offered any explanation of the Excelsiors' handling of Creighton. Why was Hannegan removed after one inning and why didn't Creighton start the game? It is possible that Hannegan was ill or out of shape. But it is unclear what effect this would have had on the Unions' conscience.

This is what the *Daily Eagle* meant. Like Creighton, Hannegan was fast and difficult to hit, but unlike Creighton he was wild—so wild that his games turned into boring waiting contests, with batters declining to swing at pitch after unreachable pitch. Without any kind of strike zone, all that opposing batters could do about it was to complain. The influential Chadwick, who later served on baseball's rules committee, railed against clubs who countered Creighton with wild hard throwers, turning the game into an unwatchable farce. He called out the Unions specifically for using Hannegan. The Unions felt justified in pitching Hannegan against Creighton because they could not handle Creighton's speed. It was tit for tat. And when Creighton surprised them by not pitching, they substituted a slower pitcher out of fairness.

The game stories leave us asking one final question: why did the game stop after six innings? According to the *New York Clipper*, the game took only two hours. It did not rain in Brooklyn on October 14th. The sun set at 5:20 PM, which would seem to allow plenty of time for nine innings. Twenty runs in six innings were not a lot in 1862, and games rarely took three hours. Besides, neither the *Clipper* nor the *Daily Eagle* mentions rain or darkness—or any other reason why the game was shortened—which they normally did in game stories. A dark possibility remains. On October 18th, the news broke that James

Creighton had left the October 14th game after gravely injuring himself. In terrible pain, he had been carried straight to his home at 307 Henry Street, where after four days of suffering he died, sending a wave of shock through the New York sports world and across the country. If the Unions and Excelsiors did not want to finish the game after seeing their friend—and baseball's greatest star—carried off the field with what must have been an appalling injury, it is not hard to understand why.

At this point, the story of James Creighton and his untimely death veers off course. We know his cause of death. His death certificate states that he died of "strangulation of intestine." The death certificate was signed by Creighton's doctor, John Byrne, who incidentally was a friend and colleague of Dr. Joseph Jones, the president of the Excelsior baseball club.

They say in the military that the first reports are always wrong (and they should know). James Creighton's cause of death was reported in newspapers across the country as, among other things, a rupture of the spleen, a rupture of the bladder, a heart attack, unspecified internal injuries and an abdominal injury caused by a mighty swing of the bat. The *Boston Daily Advertiser* of October 22, 1862, reported that "The well-known baseball player of Brooklyn, James Creighton, who was the swiftest and the most efficient pitcher in the United States, burst a blood vessel in striking at a ball in a match played on Wednesday last [*sic*], and died in consequence on Saturday." No one in baseball seems to have tried to correct any of these stories, and it appears that no one ever publicly gave the real medical facts of Creighton's death.

There was one thing, however, that the baseball establishment, which included the sporting press, was eager to correct: the perception that baseball was responsible for the premature death of this popular athlete. The October 25, 1862, *New York Clipper* reported that Creighton's death was caused not by anything that happened in the Unions game, but "by internal injuries, resulting from a severe strain he received while batting a ball in the last match played between the Willow and St. George cricket clubs on Oct. 7th." Shortly afterward,

Excelsiors President Dr. Jones announced that he wished to "correct a misstatement that has been promulgated" by pointing out that Creighton had been fatally injured in the cricket match, not in the October 14th baseball game. Henry Chadwick and the rest of baseball stuck to this story for years.

Lies can be more significant than the truth because truth lacks intent. Lies have a purpose; they tell us what others want us to believe — or not to believe, which is revealing. In 1862 baseball was a rising young sport full of ambition to conquer America. It saw cricket, which was widely played throughout the United States, as its chief competitor. Because one of baseball's selling points was that it was good for your health, the last thing it needed was to be held responsible for the death of Creighton. Baseball as an institution was attempting to shift the blame for the death of its first national star onto another sport.

As we will see, this was not the only reason why baseball and the Excelsiors were less than transparent about how James Creighton died.

With the passage of time, cricket's popularity in America plateaued and declined. The utility of blaming it for Creighton's death faded. But Creighton's story was too compelling to leave unembellished. According to the September 16, 1865, Brooklyn *Daily Eagle*, "In *one of the games* [italics added] with the Union Club, Hannegan was pitching for the Unions, and Creighton was at bat. Hannegan was joking with Jim and told him he would strike out. Creighton had struck [i.e., swung] twice, and in making a third attempt at the ball struck with great force and immediately fell down. After a while he felt no more uneasiness and played the balance of the game. But alas! He had ruptured some of the internal organs." There may be some truth behind this anecdote, but Creighton did not strike out in the October 14th game. This bit of trash talk either happened in a different Unions-Excelsiors game — or not at all.

In 1887, a man calling himself "Old Timer" wrote a letter to the St. Louis *Republican* newspaper in which he claimed to have been present as a boy at Creighton's final baseball game. "Creighton's death," it read, "occurred from a rupture of his bladder... Creighton played out the game, although I think he changed positions and went out to the field to play during the last two or three innings. Some of my companions averred that they heard his bladder burst, but if they did, they did not say anything about it at the time." Henry Chadwick himself responded by trotting out the old cricket story. "I saw Creighton play in a cricket match at Bedford...as a member of the St. George Club, in a game with the Willow Club eleven in 1862, and in that match, Creighton unknowingly ruptured himself. On that occasion Creighton said that he had strained himself playing cricket. He went home early that day from the ball match, and the next thing I heard of him was that he had died from the neglected injury he had received in the cricket match...." A medical factcheck is in order here. It is impossible to rupture an otherwise healthy bladder by swinging a bat; this would require a powerful direct blow—the kind of trauma that would come from a severe beating, a fall from height or a car accident.

"Old Timer" gives another intriguing detail from a different Excelsiors game. "I was close to Creighton one day," he wrote, "when someone said the club would have to get a substitute for Pearshall [meaning Pearsall], the first baseman. I remember Creighton's answer, which, in the light of subsequent events, proved so prophetic: 'What can't be cured must be endured.'" This is poignant because Creighton knew—as we now know—that he was already suffering from the chronic condition that would kill him.

But what uncurable affliction did Creighton's friend and teammate Aleck Pearsall have? This conversation happened around September of 1862. That was when the news broke that President Abraham Lincoln intended to issue the Emancipation Proclamation and to begin freeing the slaves. Up to that point, Lincoln's public position was that he opposed slavery in principle but was not planning any immediate action against it. Abolition was a dealbreaker for the many Northerners who supported the Union cause, but who were pro-slavery. The Excelsiors' star first baseman Aleck Pearsall was one of them. Feeling betrayed by Lincoln, he abandoned his medical practice, travelled to the South with a group of friends (including at least one other prominent baseball player) and joined the Confederate army. James Creighton grew up in America's only racially mixed neighborhood with a brother who supported Abraham Lincoln and the Union cause. The incurable affliction that James Creighton was talking about may have been the racism that led Pearsall to betray his country.

By the beginning of the twentieth century, everyone except for Henry Chadwick had stopped blaming cricket for James Creighton's death—and everyone including Chadwick continued to get the story wrong. Albert Spalding's 1911 book *America's National Game* includes the following tale, first told years after the fact by supposed eyewitness Jack Chapman, a contemporary of Creighton who played for the Brooklyn Atlantics. "I was present at the game between the Excelsiors and the Unions... at which Jim Creighton injured himself," Chapman said. "He did it in hitting out a home run. When he had crossed the rubber [home plate] he turned to George Flanley and said, 'I must have snapped my belt,' and George said, 'I guess not.' [sic?] It turned out that he had suffered a fatal injury." Spalding's best-selling book was baseball's first real history, and its impact on how early baseball is remembered was massive. Baseball histories and references are still repeating this story today.

The Chapman account may be, as MLB's witty official historian John Thorn likes to say, a fact "too good to check," but it cannot be true. Creighton did not hit a home run in the October 14th game; he hit four doubles. He had hit a memorable long homer ("over the railroad tracks") in the previous Unions-Excelsiors game, played in July 1862. It is understandable that Chapman might have mixed up the two games, but that casts doubt on the rest of his account. Even worse, the Chapman story has helped to obscure the two most important facts about the death of James Creighton. One is that he died not from a traumatic injury suffered in either the cricket match or the baseball game; he died from a chronic condition. The other is that it had nothing to do with hitting.

Life before the Civil War in the Five Points, the New York City slum where James Creighton was born and raised. The painting shows the neighborhood's unique racial mix, so-called "groceries" (shops selling hard liquor), prostitution, a robbery, streets filled with wild pigs feeding on garbage — and well-dressed gentlemen "slumming."

3 MADE IN THE USA

THE SAME AMERICA that made baseball made James Creighton. Creighton and the sport of baseball were born in the same city at about the same time. They grew up together, succeeded together and made history together. Baseball's essential appeal is that it gives us heroes. James Creighton was the first.

When Creighton was born in 1841, baseball was as far from being a national sport as it could be; it was played on the southern end of the island of Manhattan, where Creighton's family lived. It would have been hard to find anyone outside of New York State who had heard of baseball. When he died 21 years later, people were playing it in every one of the United States. It was already known as the national pastime. Baseball travelled most of its evolutionary journey from obscure folk game to national sport in the twenty-one years that James Creighton was alive.

James Creighton's twenty-one years were a dark time for New York and other cities. Nineteenth-century America was a young country that was embarking on a radical democratic experiment. Our national identity was a project very much under construction. In the late 1840s and 1850s, that project was disrupted by an immense wave of Irish Catholic and other immigrants, which sparked a powerful backlash toward anything or anyone foreign. No target was too small. Creighton was eight when the Astor Place riot happened. A rivalry between two actors, amplified by anti-Englishness, ended with hundreds of unarmed New Yorkers being shot down in the street.

When driving around New York City, I used to wonder why there were so many castle-like state militia armories in urban neighborhoods.

Who puts a military base in the inner city? I did not have to spend much time with newspapers from the 1850s before I found out. The original purpose of state militias (now the National Guard) was to defend against foreign enemies, but in times of civil disorder they were deployed against their fellow citizens. This was a regular occurrence in New York during James Creighton's boyhood. The year Creighton turned sixteen, 1857, saw an economic depression that caused bank failures, mass unemployment, hunger and violent protests. In the summer of 1857, James Creighton was living around the corner from the bloody Dead Rabbits riot, the inspiration for Martin Scorsese's 2002 film *Gangs of New York*. The Dead Rabbits riot was a spinoff from a street brawl between two rival New York City police forces—one controlled by the state government in Albany and the other by New York City's mayor. Young James witnessed brutal pogroms against African Americans; anti-slavery rallies broken up by thugs; immigrants forming their own militias to protect their communities; and angry mobs ransacking the mansions of the wealthy.

Questions of national identity played out in the world of sports, as they sometimes do. There were no professional team sports in Creighton's America, but there were games. In New York, athletically inclined adults with time on their hands played both the English sport of cricket and a homegrown game they called "base ball," which was the ancestor of modern baseball. Many early baseball players played both. Americans in other cities played cricket too, as well as their own now-extinct bat and ball games. As American prosperity created more leisure in the 1840s and 1850s, the idea began to take hold that a national sport could help unify a culturally, economically and geographically fragmented America. The choice came down to cricket versus baseball; ordinary Americans chose baseball. The excitement created by James Creighton and the 1860 Excelsiors was one of the reasons.

Baseball was native-born. So was Creighton, but he was the child of immigrants. His parents came to New York around 1820. His father, James Creighton, Sr., was an Irish Protestant born around 1790 in

County Donegal. He crossed the Atlantic after a potato crop failure—a preview of the big one—that ruined the regional economy. In New York he married Jane McBrien, also an Irish Protestant, who had come from County Sligo, probably for the same reason.

The city that the Creightons emigrated to was, like the rest of the United States, overwhelmingly native-born and Protestant. New York is synonymous with diversity today, but in the early nineteenth century it was a city haunted by fear of the Old World, the culturally strange, the non-English-speaking, and the non-white. American diversity was mainly limited to race and skin color. Ten to 15 percent of its native-born Protestants were African Americans and the US was home to several hundred thousand Native Americans. Of course, almost none of them had the right to vote. Neither did women, white or otherwise. The immigration backlash fueled a political movement called Nativism, which was born in dissent over who belonged in America and what it meant to be American. Nativism elected mayors, governors and presidents. As in 1857, it also produced terrible outbursts of violence. Ground zero was the poor urban neighborhoods full of new immigrants—neighborhoods like the one in Manhattan where the Creightons lived.

Nativists were worried that foreign powers and foreign ideas posed a threat to their infant democracy. This was not an unreasonable fear, considering that the United States was not then a world power, and that the existing world powers were hostile to democracy. In the living memory of many New Yorkers, the King of England had sent the world's greatest military across the Atlantic—twice—to bombard and occupy American cities. In 1814 British troops burned down the White House. Like today's anti-immigrant politicians, the Nativists of the mid-nineteenth century feared that democracy would fail if foreigners accustomed to taking orders from princes and popes were allowed to participate.

James Creighton's older brother John was a Nativist. He began in politics as a foot soldier in Isaiah Rynders's Empire Club. Rynders was a Democratic political leader who employed hardball tactics like

The Sixth New York Regiment was recruited from the toughest New York City neighborhoods by James Creighton's older brother John, seated at right.

voter intimidation and voter suppression against enemies ranging from the Whig party to Catholics. He supported slavery and opposed Abolitionism. Rynders and his gangs of so-called "shoulder hitters" were credited with stealing the votes that made James K. Polk president in 1844. But John Creighton seems to have been neither an anti-Catholic bigot nor a racist. For example, when the Civil War began, he broke with Democratic Tammany Hall to support the Union. Creighton was a lieutenant colonel in the Sixth New York Regiment, which was made up of Irish and German immigrants, and which was the first Union army unit to have a Catholic chaplain. Later in the war, Creighton tried to recruit volunteers for an African American unit in Brooklyn, which makes sense only if he had friends in the African American community.

In the early days of the republic, Nativists' number-one bogeyman was the Roman Catholic church, the ancient enemy of Protestantism itself. Like antisemitism in modern East Asia, it began as an abstract hatred. Before the 1830s and 1840s Catholics were rarer in New York, Philadelphia and Boston than Buddhists are in those cities now. In 1820, the year James Creighton, Sr. crossed the Atlantic Ocean, the five-year-old St. Patrick's Cathedral—the first one, on Mulberry Street—was one of only two Catholic churches in the entire city of New York. There was not a single Catholic church in Brooklyn or anywhere in Long Island, New Jersey, Massachusetts or Connecticut.

The Creightons lived and worked just north of City Hall in lower Manhattan. James Creighton's first home was in a Sixth Ward slum called the Five Points, which took its name from an asymmetrical intersection near what is now Foley Square in Manhattan. The neighborhood was uniquely diverse for early nineteenth-century New York, which may explain John Creighton's unusual open-mindedness. It had a small Irish Catholic minority even before the Great Famine. The Five Points neighborhood was developed in the early 1800s on the site of the Collect Pond, a body of water spoiled by decades of runoff from tanneries that were then located well north of the city. As New York expanded, swallowing up more and more of Manhattan Island, real estate developers buried the pond under landfill, but wetlands are wet for a reason. The area remained damp and flood-prone, and the buildings they built there had an alarming tendency to sink. The Sixth Ward attracted residents with no affordable other options—the poor, the downtrodden, and struggling recent immigrants.

In 1829, James Creighton, Sr. begins to appear in New York City directories at 108 Anthony Street and, later, 48 Anthony. Later renamed Worth Street to cleanse it of bad associations, Anthony Street was one of the streets that intersected at the infamous Five Points. Creighton is listed in various city directories as manager of a porterhouse or as the keeper of a porter and cider vault. Like others in the alcohol business, James Creighton, Sr. was useful to Tammany Hall. He hosted meetings, did political errands and provided the Democratic party with polling places.

There is no doubt that the young Creighton grew up playing baseball and, although no records of high school sports from that time have survived, we know that they existed. In the 1840s baseball was already an old game in New York. It had been popular among children and students for decades, probably longer than that. New York City's Knickerbocker Club, which conventional baseball histories wrongly call the first adult baseball club, was founded in 1845. There is a lot we do not know about baseball before the Knickerbockers. Unfortunately for baseball historians (and biographers), James Creighton grew up during baseball's Dark Ages. Before the 1850s, we know that there were regular pickup baseball games, as well as more organized clubs, but because newspapers of that time did not cover sports, we have almost no game stories or box scores. We have little idea who the players were, and we cannot always be sure what the game they called baseball looked like in any real detail.

When James, Jr. was eight, his mother Jane died from what her doctors called "cerebral congestion," a catchall diagnosis that could have meant almost anything. Jane Creighton was buried in a single grave in the public section, the cheapest burial option in Brooklyn's Green-Wood cemetery, which was presumably all that James Creighton, Sr. could afford. The next day, however, Creighton came up with the $110 to buy a family plot. Jane's body was exhumed and reburied there. The 60-year-old and widowered James Creighton, Sr. then moved, with eldest son John, 22, daughter Mary Ann, 15, and James, Jr., 8, into the house of John Iliffe, an English-born cobbler who lived nearby. The likely reason is that he needed Mrs. Iliffe to care for young James and his sister. In 1852, when Mary Ann Creighton was old enough to care for her younger brother, the family returned to 48 Anthony Street.

By the year 1852 the immigration tidal wave caused by the Irish Potato Famine had crested. In the six years previous, a total of one million ragged, hungry Irish peasants had stepped off boats in New York—a city that in 1845 had a population of under 400,000. Enough of them stayed to raise the city's population to 590,000 in 1850 and 1,068,000 in 1860. In 1855 an astounding one-third of New Yorkers were Irish-born. The impact this had on the city and on James Creighton's neighborhood is hard to overstate. When Creighton was in his early teens, the Sixth Ward and the adjacent Fourth Ward—once populated almost entirely by native-born Americans—had become the most populous Irish urban communities on earth.

Not only were most of the white residents of the Five Points Irish, but many spoke Gaelic as their first or only language. The embarrassing modern leprechaun, an image that is impossible to escape in America on St. Patrick's Day, originates in caricatures of the fresh-off-the-boat Irish, who struck Americans as ape-like. One lasting product of the Five Points cultural and racial mix is African American slang, which to this day is full of words borrowed from Gaelic. "Dig" in the sense of understand, for instance, is derived from the Gaelic root "tuig." Another is tap dancing, which began as an African American take on Irish step dancing; its origins can be traced to a particular nightclub on Orange Street and a particular performer, Master Juba, whom Charles Dickens took on tour in the UK. Orange was another of the streets that intersected at the Five Points.

The 1855 New York State census paints a grim picture of James Creighton's neighborhood after it became predominantly Irish. A vast prostitution industry recruited the native-born poor and desperate immigrants. The making and selling of alcohol, James Creighton, Sr.'s business, was the Sixth Ward's second biggest employer. About a quarter of the buildings on Anthony Street housed ground-floor taverns or shops selling homemade liquor; these were known euphemistically as "groceries." Judging by the police blotter, drunkenness, brawls and sex crimes were common. On one census page from the Creighton's block of Anthony Street we find several brothels, whose inhabitants include Ellen Hughes, 17, born in Ireland, and New York–born Elizabeth Dusenberry, age 14. Both had "prostitution" listed as their occupation. In 1855 New York, the police sometimes arrested street prostitutes, but working in a brothel was perfectly legal. In the 1880s, the legal age of sexual consent was raised to 16 years old—from 10.

The thrill of vice and the exotic racial climate of the Five Points attracted public curiosity; many a pulp novel was set there. It also attracted tourists. Young James Creighton would have seen guided "slumming parties" walking through his neighborhood, accompanied by bodyguards and gawking at urban poverty and interracial couples and their families going about their daily lives. In 1842 novelist Charles Dickens came to New York and went slumming. You might think that a resident of Victorian London had seen everything, but a visit to the neighborhood apparently shocked Dickens, who wrote: "Here, too are lanes and alleys paved with mud, knee deep… underground chambers, where they dance and game… hideous tenements which take their name from robbery and murder [one infamous tenement was called 'Bandit's Roost']; all that is loathsome, drooping, and decayed is here."

The Nativist backlash against mass immigration radically altered New York City's culture, economy and politics. It also affected the world of sports. In May 1851 a gang of "short boys," or young Nativist thugs, crossed the Hudson River from New York to Hoboken, New Jersey to attack Germans who were picnicking with their families at the Elysian Fields, a private park with baseball and cricket grounds. There were several fatalities and hundreds were wounded. One German was shot in the groin by Michael McCarty, a member of the Knickerbocker baseball club and manager of the Colonnade, a restaurant and bar where baseball clubs kept dressing rooms. Surprisingly, this incident appears in the Knickerbocker baseball club's scorebooks, which are preserved in the New York Public Library. The Knickerbockers game of May 26 lasted only four innings before being, according to a handwritten note, "broken up by the Dutch fight."

Nativism fed the rise of baseball. It was one of the reasons why Americans felt they needed a national sport, but it was the main reason why that sport had to be homegrown. In the 1907 edition of his book *How to Become a Base-Ball Player*, John Ward tells of interviewing William F. Ladd, an original member of the Knickerbocker club in the 1840s, about the origins of baseball. "Mr. Ladd [told me]," Ward writes, "that the reason they chose the game of Base Ball instead of — and in fact in opposition to — cricket was because they regarded Base Ball as a purely American game; and it appears that there was at that time some considerable prejudice against adopting any game of foreign invention." In the 1840s Nativist firebrand Mike Walsh, who represented the Creighton's neighborhood in Congress, proclaimed that if he were elected mayor, he would play baseball in City Hall Park every Sunday. To Walsh, playing the people's homegrown game was a political statement—a two-fingered salute to the cricket-playing English and a middle finger to the anglophile American upper classes. Like many young men of his generation, the poet and journalist Walt Whitman was both a Nativist and a passionate advocate of baseball. Baseball was rising in popularity on its own in the 1840s, but its evolution into a modern sport was turbocharged by the anti-immigrant backlash of the 1850s. If you search digitized American newspaper databases for the phrases "national game" and "national sport," you will find virtually nothing before the year 1854. A year or two later, however, both phrases—and the idea behind them—are everywhere. Eighteen-fifty-four was the year that the American Party, known better by its nickname the "Know-Nothings," became a national political force.

Immigration and its effects also advanced the cause of baseball by driving native-born, baseball-playing New Yorkers out of the city. Baseball left the island of Manhattan in different ways at different times by different routes, but it went wherever New Yorkers went. The earliest baseball clubs that we know much about were the Knickerbockers, the Gothams and the Eagles. They were made up mostly of white-collar workers who lived in Manhattan. Baseball was also played by New York's butchers, fish dealers and grocers, who worked in great public markets like Manhattan's Washington Market and the Fulton Fish Market. They had only one thing in common with the bankers and stockbrokers of the Knickerbocker Club or the printers and journalists of the Eagle Club—ample leisure time. Starting in the 1840s, real estate development robbed the Knickerbockers and the others of one after another of the open spaces where they had played. They relocated across the Hudson River to the Elysian Fields in Hoboken, New Jersey, which were reachable by ferry from New York City's financial district. There baseball flourished in a kind of greenhouse, enjoying adequate air, space and light apart from the dirty, dangerous and crowded city. The desire of New Yorkers to seek peace and safety—and to get away from poverty, immigrants, crime and disorder—also drove the creation of the earliest New York suburbs. The people who created these early suburbs were native-born New Yorkers. One of the first things they did when they arrived was to start a baseball club. An example is the Union Club, founded in 1855 in Morrisania. Today, Morrisania is an inner-city neighborhood in the South Bronx, but in the mid-nineteenth century it was a fashionable suburban development. In the center of it was a railroad station and a baseball field. The Excelsiors of Brooklyn Heights were also founded by suburban pioneers from Manhattan. Lack of space and alienation from the city also drove whole communities and industries to expand beyond the city or to abandon it altogether. As New York City's population exploded, so did that of nearby Brooklyn, and so did the industry that fed both. The Atlantics of Brooklyn, the Amateur Era's greatest dynasty, began as a pickup game played by butchers, fish dealers and other market traders from a public market.

Native-born African Americans also brought baseball with them when they left New York City. The racial violence of the early and mid-nineteenth century drove African Americans across the East River to Brooklyn—so many that, as the population of New York City rose exponentially in the 1850s and 1860s, the African American population declined in absolute numbers. The reason was not economics; it was fear. Some of these refugees founded baseball clubs in new or expanding African American communities in Weeksville, now Bedford-Stuyvesant, and Williamsburg. The African American Unknown Club of Weeksville played a match against the African American Monitors of Williamsburg at Bedford in 1862. This was a big enough game that it was covered by the white press. For that reason, we know the names of the players as well as the score.

New York City's shipyards and related businesses were originally located near Corlear's Hook on the Manhattan side of the East River. They employed shipwrights, dock builders, iron workers, carpenters, ropemakers and sailmakers. In the 1840s and 1850s the entire industry began to move across the river to Greenpoint and Williamsburg, bringing thousands of baseball-playing New Yorkers to what in 1854 became the Eastern District of Brooklyn. Among them were the founders of the Eckford baseball club, the champions of baseball in 1862 and 1863.

Baseball did not evolve from a local folk game into a national sport gradually. It happened in a flash. In 1854, Judge William Van Cott of the Gotham baseball club wrote a letter to the principal New York City newspapers talking up the game as a serious adult sport. "Sir," he writes, "...there are now in this city three regularly organized clubs." Games between these clubs attracted the first stirrings of public and media interest in baseball. In 1855 Van Cott and his brother Thomas called for a convention of baseball clubs to establish guidelines for interclub play and to standardize the rules, but the convention failed. The reason was that baseball's most prestigious club, the Knickerbockers, did not choose to attend. In September of the following year, however, the Knickerbockers had an attitude adjustment. A September 1856 game between the Gothams and Knickerbockers had attracted an unusual amount of gambling action. Just before the first pitch, a ringer arrived in the form of pitcher and infielder Joseph Pinckney. "Some dissatisfaction," understated *Porter's Spirit of the Times*, a national sporting weekly, "was expressed by members of the Knickerbocker club and their outside friends [i.e., bettors], at the introduction of Mr. Pinckney, a superior player, from the Union club of Morrisania into the club of the Gothams for this occasion..." The Gothams plus one beat the Knickerbockers badly, 21–7. The Knickerbockers suddenly agreed not only to attend but to host a general convention of New York-area baseball clubs. Given baseball's fraught historical relationship with gambling, it is ironic that baseball's first step toward a national organization was set in motion by a gambling scandal, although it becomes less ironic with each passing season.

In late January 1857 a credible baseball convention was held in a New York City hotel. Fourteen clubs attended, all from in or around New York City and Brooklyn. They decided to make it an annual event. The 1858 convention established a governing body, which put baseball's national ambitions front and center. Even though 21 of the 22 clubs that came to the 1858 convention were from New York State, they adopted the aspirational, if not ridiculous, name the "National Association of Base Ball Players." The NABBP is the direct ancestor of today's Organized Baseball. But calling baseball "national" did not make it so. Baseball needed the drama of competition and rivalry to capture the interest of Americans beyond the Elysian Fields and Manhattan. It found that drama in Brooklyn.

In 1873, Henry Chadwick remembered how and when that happened. "[In 1854] nines used to play on Wheat Hill [the future site of the Union Grounds, the first ballpark], at Williamsburg, and at Bedford. in 1855...the sport, which had grown into favor at Hoboken for years previous, found its way to Brooklyn [proper], and the Continental and Harmony Clubs were organized, and afterward the noted Atlantic." Visitors to Brooklyn in the late 1850s were struck by the sight of an entire city in the grip of baseball mania. Brooklyn had something to prove, and competition took precedence over exercise. It also had lots of young men and lots of space. Brooklynites founded new clubs every week, and the first thing these clubs did was to challenge another club. The Excelsiors began in 1854, and the Atlantics, Eckfords and Putnams in 1855. Baseball games started to draw spectators. In greater and greater numbers, Brooklynites went to ballgames not simply to watch but to root. The drama of clubs from underdog Brooklyn trying to beat the big, bad New Yorkers at their own game added extra interest. Given more and more coverage by the New York–based sports weeklies, baseball's first intercity rivalry captured the imagination of the country. Brooklyn youth baseball served as a massive reservoir of playing talent that fed the adult clubs. The best of Brooklyn — the Atlantics, Eckfords and Excelsiors — reached competitive parity with their New York City counterparts in only three years.

In the early 1900s Henry Chadwick argued a theory that baseball had originated in England and came here with early immigrants. But this is what Chadwick said about the subject way back in 1868: "The game of baseball may be said to date its origin [to] 1857."

The year 1857 was packed with historical turning points, baseball and otherwise. Economic disasters, riots and class conflict convulsed New York and the country. The national schism over slavery had destroyed the Whig party, created the Republican party, and was driving the nation toward Civil War. Nativism's craziest project, William Walker's illegal invasion of Nicaragua using American volunteers, ended in bloody defeat in 1857. James Creighton, Jr.'s elder brother John was one of Walker's few competent officers. He returned home and was promptly arrested for interfering in US foreign policy. His Tammany Hall friends got him off. Back in New York, the alcohol industry was in retreat. Temperance advocates exploited Nativist stereotypes of hard-drinking, violent Irish and beery Germans to pass harsh state liquor laws in 1854. The new laws severely restricted the sale of alcohol and closed hundreds of Manhattan breweries, shops and bars. The new laws were a personal disaster for James Creighton, Sr., putting him out of business entirely. The 1855 New York State census lists James Creighton, Sr.'s occupation as "bootmaker."

The year 1857 was also the year that baseball made its great leap from a game to a sport. The backlash against immigration had strengthened baseball at the expense of cricket. The farther-seeing members of the American sporting community could tell which way the wind was blowing. Harry Wright was an English-born cricketer with a well-paid position on New York City's St. George Cricket Club, but he realized that baseball was the future. After switching sports, Wright went on to create the job of baseball manager, lead the 1869 Cincinnati Red Stockings to their epic undefeated season, pave the way for the first national baseball league, manage professionally for 25 years, and earn a plaque in Cooperstown. Wright first picked up a baseball bat when he joined a Knickerbockers game at the Elysian Fields in 1857. Eighteen-fifty-seven was the year that baseball formed a governing body and established rules including nine-inning games, nine-man teams and 90-foot basepaths. It was the year that the game proclaimed its ambition to become the national sport. It was the year that George Wilkes made the weekly *Spirit of the Times* the first national sports newspaper to give baseball precedence over cricket. In 1857 the epicenter of the baseball world moved from New York City to the other side of the East River. It was also the year that James Creighton moved to Brooklyn.

The two faces of Brooklyn as viewed from New York Harbor in the decades before the Civil War — grand houses on the Heights and the docks and warehouses of the Brooklyn business district below.

4 The Infant Phenomenon

Every account of James Creighton's life starts with the same lie. Creighton did not live long enough to tell his own story. Sportswriters and historians have relied on the following brief bio that appears, with slight variations, in nineteenth-century newspapers.

"James Creighton was born in New York city...[as] a child his parents removed him to Brooklyn, where they...resided.... Creighton took a great interest in the game, and with the assistance of several others, started a little club which was known as the Young America, which, however, lasted but a brief season. He next assisted in starting the Niagara Club, for whom he played second base, George Flanley, now captain of the Excelsior club...playing short stop. They played many matches in which they were successful, which gave them such a confidence in their prowess that they resolved to play the Star Club, then the crack Junior Club, and it was in this match that Creighton gave evidence of those qualities that afterwards made him so renowned."

James Creighton was not a child when he moved to Brooklyn. He was born in lower Manhattan in 1841 and lived there until late 1857, when he was 16 years old and already an outstanding athlete. Young America was a common name for Amateur Era baseball clubs, but there is no evidence that Creighton helped found or played for any of them. It is even less likely that he had anything to do with founding the Niagara Club of Brooklyn. He did play for the Niagaras, but that club was formed before Creighton came to Brooklyn. These are odd errors to make, considering how small the baseball world was in Creighton's time. Everybody knew everybody, especially in New York and Brooklyn. But getting the timing of James Creighton's relocation to Brooklyn wrong was not a mistake. It was done on purpose.

The baseball rulebook is not exactly summer beach reading, but if you approach it the right way—paying attention to what is there and what is not there, and when—it is surprising what you can learn. If baseball writes a rule against something, to take an obvious example, then somebody must have been doing it. No one proposed outlawing an infielder getting on his hand and knees and blowing a ground ball into foul territory, for example, until the late Lenny Randle of the Seattle Mariners did it in a game 1991. The oldest baseball rules that survive (they were not the first!) were written by the Knickerbocker Club in 1845 and published in 1848. At that time, baseball was an amateur sport, but the 1848 Knickerbocker rules say nothing about amateurism or about money at all. There is no rule forbidding clubs from paying their players and there is no rule against players or even umpires betting on games. This tells us one of two things: either these behaviors were approved of in the 1840s, or they were unknown. The answer is probably one of each; no one had a problem with gambling, and paying players was unheard of.

Professionalism was first addressed by the baseball rules of 1859, when James Creighton was playing for the Niagara Club. That year a sentence was added to the rules that reads, "No person who received compensation for his services as a player shall be competent to play in any match." The obvious inference is that around 1858 some baseball clubs were beginning to pay their players in some way and that this was seen as a problem. The late 1850s saw more interclub play, rivalries between clubs, communities and cities, and growing public interest. An 1858 all-star baseball series between Brooklyn and New York City drew big crowds, but the real news was that they were the first paying crowds. The rule makers of 1859 were responding to a new phenomenon in baseball, fandom, that raised the competitive stakes in baseball and threatened to bring serious money into the sport.

The Knickerbockers and the older New York City clubs were not above placing a bet, and they enjoyed friendly rivalries with the few clubs they considered their friends and social equals, but they had zero interest in selling tickets, entertaining strangers or winning championships. They played the game seriously, but they did not develop, recruit or pursue talent from other clubs. From the beginning, Brooklyn was different. The first Brooklyn club, the Excelsiors, was founded in 1854 by men who, at first glance, look like the Knickerbockers. Most of the first Excelsiors were New Yorkers who had bought homes in Brooklyn, intending to commute to work. The founding membership of the Excelsiors is a cross-section of striving, successful New Yorkers, including Wall Street heavy hitters and medical doctors who were classmates at Columbia with members of the Knickerbockers. They had friends, colleagues and even relatives among the Knickerbockers. Choosy about opponents, the Knickerbockers rarely came to Brooklyn but when they did, it was always to play the Excelsiors or one of their affiliated clubs. The Excelsiors treated the Knickerbockers with the deference of a younger brother to an older brother. The special relationship between the two clubs is the true subject of the famous double team portrait taken on the field before a game in August 1859. Excelsiors Club president Dr. Joseph Jones, standing at center in top hat and tails, is holding the game ball. The custom in amateur baseball was that the winning team took home the game ball as a trophy. The Excelsiors won this game, 20–5, but afterward they presented the ball to the Knickerbockers as a

Sporting a top hat and holding the game ball in this 1859 photograph is Dr. Joseph B. Jones, president of the Excelsiors and architect of the legendary 1860 club built around catcher Joe Leggett and pitcher James Creighton.

show of respect. The two clubs remained close years after the Excelsiors became championship contenders and the Knickerbockers became a living museum of early baseball.

As similar as the original Excelsiors and Knickerbockers might seem, the two clubs had different ideas about what the game of baseball was for. The Excelsiors were founded as the Jolly Young Bachelors, but almost immediately changed their name to Excelsior, roughly Latin for "onward and upward." "Excelsior" is the New York State motto, which comes from a poem by Longfellow, but the new name also reflects a change in club philosophy—from playing for the camaraderie and the fun of it à la the Knickerbockers to an ambition to build and grow the sport. In October 1857, the Excelsiors added Dr. Joseph Jones from the Esculapian Club, which was made up of medical men, and merged with the Wayne Club, acquiring star catcher Joseph Leggett, Richard Oliver and James Bach. These men were active promoters of baseball; they umpired games in distant cities (Amateur Era umpires were usually active players from an outside club chosen by both sides); helped spread the game beyond New York; and held club and national offices. The Excelsiors normally held officer elections in April, but in 1857 they met in November, five months early, to elect new members Joseph Jones and Joe Leggett as president and vice-president. The reason for the urgency was to have new leadership in place for the important first annual baseball convention of 1858 that was scheduled for March. Jones and Leggett were allies and, given their involvement in physical training and weightlifting, very likely knew each other before Leggett joined the Excelsiors. On Wednesday evening, March 10, 1858, Jones and Leggett walked into the Gotham tavern at 298 Bowery in Manhattan, where the opening session of the convention was held, with a new, expansionist agenda for the Excelsiors and for baseball itself. The assembled representatives of the principal adult clubs of New York and Brooklyn passed a motion by Dr. Jones to establish a five-man committee to draft rules for future meetings. They put Joe Leggett on the rules committee. Jones was then elected first vice-president of the new National Association of Base Ball Players, baseball's first governing body; in 1860 he became president.

Joseph Jones was a man with a bold plan. Ordinary baseball clubs in the 1850s played for fun and exercise. The better clubs were in it for glory; they played to beat other clubs and, later in the decade, to win championships. Dr. Jones's Excelsiors had a further goal: to build a great baseball club and use it to take the New York game national. In 1860 they made their move. The 1860 Excelsiors were the finest team in baseball, and they had James Creighton, baseball's greatest player, in his prime. They made the first-ever baseball road trips, playing games across upstate New York and then the mid-Atlantic states. People in these places played bat-and-ball games of varying similarity to New York baseball, but after seeing Leggett, Flanley and Creighton at play, they converted to the New York game. The Excelsiors' missionary work on behalf of the sport took precedence even over pursuing championships. For example, in 1860 the Excelsiors played intramurally two or three days a week, along with a full slate of series against New York and Brooklyn clubs. Yet they spent a valuable resource—innings from an overworked James Creighton—on a pair of exhausting mid-season long-distance tours. In the war year of 1862 the Excelsiors played only a couple of games against other clubs, in effect abstaining from competing for the championship. But they still traveled to Boston to showcase baseball and its star attraction, the unhittable Creighton.

Joseph Jones was a veteran public health reformer and physical fitness advocate. In the 1850 US Census Jones's occupation is listed as "teacher." He was teaching physical education at his own private gymnasium at the corner of Pineapple and Fulton Streets, halfway up Brooklyn Heights from the Fulton Ferry. Jones's facility was Brooklyn's first gymnasium. Jones was ahead of his time in other ways, too; an ally of contemporary feminism, he offered classes to both sexes. (He later promoted girls' and women's baseball). In straightlaced, churchgoing Protestant Brooklyn, where you could be arrested for playing baseball on the Sabbath, prudes complained that delicate females should not work up a sweat, and that it was especially indecent for men and women to see each other jumping, stretching and lifting weights. Jones responded that the sexes were kept strictly separate at his facility. He published a testimonial from his friend Henry Ward Beecher, an advocate of exercise and, until his 1872 sex scandal, the most admired religious leader in the country.

When Jones was 30, he sold his gymnasium and entered the College of Physicians and Surgeons, or CPS, the medical school of New York's Columbia College. He went there for a medical education, but he left with an incurable case of baseball fever. This is unsurprising; Columbia students had been crazy about baseball going as far back as the eighteenth century. Joseph Jones graduated and began to practice medicine. He joined the Esculapians, a baseball club made up of doctors and medical students that played near Carroll Park in Brooklyn, before moving onward and upward to the Excelsiors. (According to a 1910 interview with a former Excelsior, the Esculapians were mocked by neighborhood boys for wearing velvet gloves to protect their valuable hands; if this is true, then these were the first baseball gloves.)

Joseph Jones later became superintendent of the Board of Education's truancy department, putting his athletic ability to use chasing down schoolchildren playing hooky. Clearly practicing what he preached about staying in shape, Jones appeared in baseball old timers' games into his 50s. In 1898, he won a borough-wide Brooklyn bowling tournament at the age of 75. According to a 1931 *Daily Eagle* article about the old Brooklyn Dispensary, "[Dr. Jones's] long white beard and lanky frame were familiar landmarks to everyone in the neighborhood. In his earlier days Dr. Jones had been a famous sporting character [and] was an accomplished boxer." They say that the last thing a boxer loses is his punch, which explains a news item from 1866. Walking home late one night, Jones was assaulted by a pair of muggers. One ran away; the other he beat so badly that, to the annoyance of the police, Jones refused to press charges.

When Jones took over the Excelsiors going into the 1858 season, they faced a mighty obstacle: the Atlantic Club, also of Brooklyn. The Excelsiors saw themselves as rivals of the Atlantics, but the Atlantics could be forgiven for not knowing that they were in a fight. The Atlantics went undefeated in 1855 and 1856; they were consensus champions in 1857. Dr. Jones's 1858 Excelsiors were improved but when they took on the Atlantics, they were crushed, 22–10 and 27–6. In 1858 the Atlantics went undefeated and once again defended their championship. In 1859 the Excelsiors declined to play the Atlantics, who nosed out the Eckfords (also of Brooklyn) to win a fifth consecutive national championship.

Jones and the Excelsiors needed a talent upgrade. Getting it would require some delicacy, because standing in the way was an unwritten tradition in baseball that social considerations trumped competition. The early Amateur Era clubs were made up of men who knew each other from the neighborhood, the workplace or the volunteer fire company—not from the ball field. They belonged to their communities in a truer and deeper way than today's professional or college teams belong to theirs. Some were made up of the better players from those communities, but it would have been pushing the ethical envelope to import players from the outside simply to improve the team. In amateur baseball, of course, there was no such thing as drafting or trading for players. Dr. Jones and the Excelsiors got creative. They had already used a club merger to acquire Joe Leggett, a terrific hitter and the finest catcher of the day. In 1858, they acquired hard-hitting John Holder from the Atlantics; we are not sure how.

The Excelsiors turned to training and player development. Leggett taught his teammates how to use weights, coached young players and scouted pickup games for talent. The Excelsiors established relationships with the Stars and the Niagaras, both junior clubs, that provided a reliable pipeline of young prospects. The Stars and Niagaras received instruction and organizational support, including access to the Excelsiors' original playing fields near Carroll Park, in exchange for sending their best players to the Excelsiors when they aged out of the junior classification. The system operated loosely like a modern professional farm system, with players maturing, improving and moving up the organizational ladder in an orderly way, normally two per year from the Niagaras to the Stars to the big club. James Creighton followed this path. In one three-year period, Asa Brainard and his brother Harrison

Brainard; brothers Charles Whiting and John Whiting; George Flanley and Creighton all graduated from the Stars and joined the Excelsiors. The Excelsiors never explicitly acknowledged this arrangement, but it was no secret. In 1859 the New York *Sunday Mercury* matter-of-factly described the junior Star Club, James Creighton, Jr.'s club, as "an offshoot from the Excelsior club."

James Creighton stands out on this list like a tourist on Fifth Avenue. He is the only player who did not belong in any sense to the Brooklyn neighborhood where the Excelsiors played and where nearly all its players grew up. A few Excelsiors were born elsewhere but came to Brooklyn for work, school or family reasons. Creighton was the only Excelsior with no non-baseball connection to Brooklyn at all, which brings us back to the why of the often-repeated falsehood that James Creighton moved to Brooklyn as a child. Its purpose was to obscure the fact that the Excelsiors had recruited him as a minor and brought him and his family to Brooklyn *from another city*. This was pushing the envelope of the values of Amateur Era baseball hard. The Excelsiors created the fiction that Creighton belonged to the community that had produced his teammates to avoid awkward questions about how they acquired Creighton—and for what.

The recruitment of Creighton raises other questions. Did the rest of baseball know about it? The answer is yes. We know this from parody song lyrics written by James Whyte Davis of the Knickerbockers for a December 1858 baseball banquet attended by some 200 players from the principal Brooklyn and New York City clubs. Davis's song devotes a stanza or two to each club. The Excelsiors section goes like this:

> First a welcome to our guests, the brave Excelsior boys,
> They play a strong and lively game, and make a lively noise;
> They buck at every club, without breaking any bones,
> Assisted by their president, the witty Doctor Jones....
> ...They have Leggett for a catcher, and who is always there,
> A gentleman in every sense, whose play is always square;
> Then Russell, Reynolds, Dayton, and also Johnny Holder,
> And the infantile "phenomenon," who'll play when he gets older.

The phrase "infantile phenomenon" comes from Charles Dickens's novel *Nicholas Nickleby*, in which a child theatrical prodigy is advertised under that name. Davis must be referring to James Creighton; there are no other plausible candidates. As this song makes clear, Creighton was already known to be an unusually talented athlete; his recruitment was an open secret; and the baseball world—including the people who made and enforced the rules—knew of the Excelsiors' quasi-farm system arrangement. If everyone in baseball knew that the Excelsiors, in effect, "owned" Creighton two years before he joined the club, it follows that they approved of this relationship. Performed only months after the Creightons changed cities, the song also suggests that the Excelsiors likely found Creighton in New York City and brought him to Brooklyn, as opposed to discovering him in Brooklyn after his family moved there for their own reasons. The Excelsiors may have discovered Creighton in a medical setting. It would not be surprising if Creighton was being treated for his hernia as a teenager; and Dr. Jones was affiliated for a time with New York Hospital, then located across the street from Creighton's home. This would also fit Dr. Jones's MO. Jones recruited Creighton's teammate Aleck Pearsall in medical school, where Jones was Pearsall's precept, or personal tutor and advisor.

Davis's 1858 song tells us something else. For more than a century, a promising baseball prospect has been called a "phenom," which also comes from Dickens's phrase, "infantile phenomenon." A search through digital databases of books, periodicals and newspapers turned up a few boxing references, but no baseball use of the terms "phenom," "infantile phenomenon" or any variation of these terms before the year 1858. Creighton was the first player we know of to be called by that name. He was the original baseball "phenom."

Dr. Jones's Excelsiors never admitted to recruiting a teenage James Creighton or bringing him to Brooklyn. Is that all they weren't admitting? Did they help or even pay James Creighton, Sr. to move his family across the East River so that young James could join the club?

In 1855, after decades in the alcohol business, James Creighton, Sr. was now working at home making shoes for a living. He lived with his son John, 26, daughter Mary Ann, 18, and son James, Jr., 12. He owned a brick house valued at $5,000, part of which he rented out to another family. At that time in America shoes were not mass-produced; like other apparel, boots and shoes were hand-made by small-time artisans, even for the poor. James Creighton, Sr. appears for the last time in a New York City directory in 1857, living at 48 Worth Street (the renamed Anthony Street). This is the profile of a man of no more than moderate means. A $5,000 brick house had value, but a middle-class or wealthier man of that time would have had servants and would not have needed to share his home with strangers to pay the bills. Remember that when Jane Creighton died in 1849, Creighton, Sr. moved in with an older couple so they could help with childcare; this certainly suggests tightened economic circumstances. In 1840s and 1850s New York City, families above poverty could afford childcare. Irish girls came cheap. Did James Creighton, Sr. come into money between 1849 and 1857? Possibly, but in 1857 New York experienced a severe economic depression, and learning a new trade in a person's late 60s seems more consistent with downward than with upward mobility.

According to Brooklyn Land Conveyance records, James Creighton, Sr. purchased a brick row house at 307 Henry Street in what is now the neighborhood of Cobble Hill and took legal possession of it on February 5th, 1858. The seller of record is a builder named John Morrison. For a head of household, the 1860 federal census lists both the value of a home and the total assets excluding the home. Number 307 Henry Street is valued at $8,000—about average for the neighborhood—and James Creighton, Sr.'s other assets come to $1,000, which is far below average. The Creightons have no live-in servants. This is unusual for the time and place. Fifty-four of the nearest 60 houses to the Creightons' have one or more servants; 28 have two or more.

It is hard to see how James Creighton, Sr. could have afforded to buy an $8,000 three-story brick row house in what was then an upscale suburban neighborhood without help. It is unlikely that the help came from his eldest son. John Creighton also came to Brooklyn in 1858, but did not move in with the rest of the family. After marrying

Sarah Phipard in October 1858, he lived with his in-laws. The erratic John Creighton struggled financially for most of his adult life. Not only is there nothing to suggest that John Creighton had the money to help his family buy the house at 307 Henry Street, but it seems more likely that any financial help would have gone in the opposite direction.

The chief suspects for the buyers of the house on Henry Street are the rich men behind the Excelsiors. The block where 307 Henry Street is located was part of a tract of farmland that was being developed and turned into blocks of fine brick and brownstone rowhouses by investors from two families, the Van Nostrands and the Suydams. These families had close business and family connections. Their money originally came from the wholesale food business, but in the 1840s and 1850s they were diversifying into finance and real estate. As part of the development, they built grand houses for themselves on Henry Street, a few doors away from number 307. In the 1850s there were three Van Nostrand or Suydam households on that block. One was headed by John Van Nostrand, 68 years old, who is listed in the 1850 census as the president of an insurance company; he owned $50,000 in real estate. Next door is Henry Suydam, 45, a grocer with $70,000 in real estate. Next door to him is James Van Nostrand, 58, a former grocer but now president of New York City's Merchants Exchange Bank, which is now J. P. Morgan Chase. (Its current president makes about $40 million dollars a year). He owned $31,000 in real estate. Living with Henry Suydam is his son John Suydam, age 19, a clerk. Two doors down in the house of his father is James Van Nostrand, Jr., also age 19 and a clerk. One afternoon in 1854, a group including John Suydam, James Van Nostrand, Jr. and a cousin went to the Elysian Fields in New Jersey to watch a baseball game between the Knickerbockers and Eagles, probably the exciting 22–21 Eagles victory of Friday, November 17. They enjoyed it so much that they decided to form Brooklyn's first baseball club, soon to be called the Excelsiors. Starting in 1857, the Excelsiors played their home games on one of a cluster of baseball diamonds that were used by the Stars, Niagaras, Esculapians, Charter Oaks, Waynes and others. These clubs were connected by social, family, business or baseball ties. The Niagaras and Stars were quasi-subsidiaries of the Excelsiors.

The Charter Oaks were an adult club that took players from the Stars and Niagaras who were not Excelsiors material.

To summarize, in early 1858 James Creighton's father moved his family into a new house in a part of Brooklyn being developed by the wealthy Suydam and Van Nostrand families. The house was on the same block as the residences of John Suydam and James Van Nostrand, two cofounders and wealthy backers of the Excelsiors. The Excelsiors were James Creighton, Jr.'s future team and the sponsor of the Brooklyn junior club that he joined in that same year. The seller who legally conveyed the house to James Creighton, Sr., builder John Morrison, was a brother-in-law of Edward Shaurman and business partners with Edward Shaurman and his cousin Nelson Shaurman. Nelson Shaurman played baseball for the Charter Oaks, who shared playing grounds with the Excelsiors; he was also a close friend of Excelsiors president Joseph Jones. Edward Shaurman is the contractor of record for several houses in the area and on that same block of Henry Street, including number 307, that were built on land owned by the Suydams and Van Nostrands. The Excelsiors were compensating Creighton and his family with real estate, conveyed through a middleman.

There is more. The Excelsiors were staunch amateurs, at least by their definition of the word. Like their mentors, the Knickerbockers, they refused to charge admission or accept a share of the gate money from an away game, even to "defray expenses." When paying players cash under the table became common in the mid-1860s, the Excelsiors publicly opposed the practice. But there are other ways to pay than in dollars. The 1865 Philadelphia Athletics, for example, were accused of giving slugger Al Reach a house as part of their effort to recruit him from Greenpoint, where he played for his hometown Eckfords. Harry Polhemus, the Brainards, the Whiting brothers and most of James Creighton's other Excelsiors teammates did not need to be paid to play baseball. The club did, however, give assistance to less well-off players, men like Joe Leggett and George Flanley. Club members used their influence to get these players promotions, sinecures and light-duty or no-show jobs. Excelsior members including Wall Street executive Gilbert Haight and wealthy real estate developer (and graduate of Columbia's medical school) Van Brunt Wyckoff took care of catcher Joseph Leggett by getting him positions with the Brooklyn Mercantile Library; the Brooklyn Fire Department; and the Brooklyn Police Department. During the Civil War, future Excelsior president and Brooklyn mayoral candidate John B. Woodward appointed Leggett as quartermaster of the Thirteenth New York State Militia Regiment. Infielder George Flanley was a kid from a humble Red Hook background whose father died young, leaving George to support his mother and siblings. He had a legitimate day job as a telegrapher, but the Excelsiors got him a promotion and a salary increase with the Brooklyn Police. It is consistent with the Excelsiors' understanding of the boundaries of amateurism that in 1860 they also arranged a no-show job for their brilliant young pitcher James Creighton, Jr., at the federal Custom House, a notorious source of political patronage jobs.

Later historians have convicted the Excelsiors *in absentia* of hypocrisy. Moral judgments become easier in retrospect, as context is lost, and fine distinctions fade away. In 1875 the *New York Clipper* wrote that "the Excelsiors in their palmy days had players in their nine who were duly compensated for their service, Creighton being in reality a professional." Even as early as the Excelsiors' upstate tour of 1860, however, there were murmurs. "The Excelsior Club of Brooklyn," wrote a Troy newspaper on July 3, 1860, "who have pretty well reduced baseball to a science, and who pay their pitcher $500 a year, are making a crusade through the provinces for the purposes of winning laurels, or losing them, with the different clubs on their way." This accusation was repeated in Rochester. It has also been repeated by modern historians, who generally omit that the next day the same Troy paper ate its words, saying that "[the Excelsiors] pitcher *does not* receive $500 a year, but he is a splendid player." If James Creighton was generally believed to have been paid in violation of the rules of baseball, however, the remarkable thing is not that a couple of upstate newspapers whose hometown baseball champions were outclassed complained that the grapes were sour. The remarkable thing is that so little was said about it.

Writing in 1866, influential baseball journalist Henry Chadwick drew a bright line between what he called "hired men" and "those whose loss of time and necessary expenses are very properly paid." For Chadwick, the ethical standard was not whether a player was compensated or helped financially by fellow club members; it was whether he was a mercenary, jumping from club to club chasing the highest bidder. "All clubs," he wrote, "who have first class players in their nines whose positions in life are not surrounded with pecuniary advantages, or who are not, in fact, well off in the world, of course take care that their players are not sufferers from sacrificing their time to sustain the playing reputation of the club of which they are prominent players. But this style of thing is...very different from 'hiring men,' or paying them so much a week for their services, just as 'professional' cricketers are paid." Thirteen years later, Chadwick felt that the line between amateurism and professionalism might not have been so bright. Before the mid-1860s "professional ballplaying," he said, "...though practically in existence to some extent...had not been prominently brought into public notice." Even later, in 1898, Chadwick wrote that professionalism was introduced "as early as 1860, in which year the Excelsior Club remunerated, (*sub rosa*), its noted pitcher, Creighton, for his services."

The relationship between the Excelsiors and Creighton (and Leggett and Flanley) does not seem to have crossed the line *as it was understood when they played*, but the line moved over time. A close reading of the deliberations of baseball's rules committee in the late 1850s suggests that it recognized a distinction between paying players *directly* in cash as opposed to *indirectly* in the form of jobs, property and favors. It also supports the idea that the primary target of the rule against player compensation may not have been payment *per se* but rather using payment to entice or hire away another club's players. After all, the Excelsiors did not make up a story to cover up their giving him a house and a job. They lied about where he grew up to cover up the fact that they recruited him. They did not poach him from another club, but recruiting itself was in an uncomfortably gray ethical area.

This is not, however, all that the Excelsiors did for James Creighton, Jr. and his family. In 1860 the Excelsiors also arranged a Custom House job for James Creighton, Jr.'s father, a 70-year-old retiree with no relevant experience or qualifications for this kind of work. This is harder to rationalize as innocent mutual assistance by club members. It gets worse. In 1859 there is no record of either Creighton working anywhere. The same is true in 1861. In fact, James Creighton, Jr.'s one year at the Custom House is the sum-total of his entire known employment history. Putting these events on a timeline, a narrative emerges. The house on Henry Street was given to the Creightons in 1858 as an inducement to move to Brooklyn, a *quid pro quo* that gave the Excelsiors quasi-ownership of young James, Jr. Creighton played for the Niagaras in 1858 and part of 1859 before graduating to the Star Club in late 1859. The Excelsiors began the 1860 season with Creighton as their pitcher. That year the Excelsiors reached their peak, coming within a few innings of dethroning the champion Atlantics. That same year they made their historic tours of upstate New York and the mid-Atlantic states. Creighton was the star attraction, pitching almost every inning of the 1860 season. Why was he paid in 1860? He was paid because he was supporting a family, because he was the best player in baseball, and because he was indispensable to the Excelsiors' project to make baseball our first national team sport.

How much was $1,000 (James, Jr.'s and James, Sr.'s combined Custom House salaries for 1860) in today's money? One way to look at it is as ⅛ of the cost of the brick rowhouse at 307 Henry Street, which was then valued at $8,000. Conveniently, Cobble Hill, Brooklyn today is roughly equivalent in value and social desirability to the area then. 307 Henry Street is still there, although with a different street number. According to online real estate websites, it would sell now for $4.25 million. One-eighth of that amount is a bit over $500,000. That would not buy you a week of Juan Soto today, but the average major leaguer did not make more than that until 1989. The first MLB player to reach $500,000 in annual salary was Mike Schmidt in 1977.

The following year the Civil War broke out and the Excelsiors, like most clubs, stopped playing inter-club games and cut down on practices. They also stopped paying. Unlike thousands of other Brooklyn ballplayers, James Creighton, Jr. did not serve in the military. He started playing cricket, a sport that was notorious among Americans for its coziness with gambling and for "paying [star players] so much a week for their services." The following year the war was still going on, but baseball began to emerge from its dormancy. Suddenly, the papers printed shocking rumors that Creighton was going to leave the Excelsiors and jump to the rival Atlantic Club. In fact, there were two sets of rumors, five months apart. Again, the timeline is significant. There were two distinct series of events. On April 7th, 1862, the Brooklyn *Daily Eagle* reported that rumors of James Creighton joining the Atlantics were untrue, "as we learn from reliable authority." On April 18th, Creighton, Flanley and Brainard played in an informal mixed game with members of the Exercise Club. On April 26th, a *New York Clipper* column that answered questions from readers stated categorically, "Mr. Creighton does not receive pay for his services as pitcher for the Excelsior Club." On June 5th, Creighton and Flanley appear on another combined team representing Brooklyn's Western District against a visiting Philadelphia combined team. On June 26th Creighton is back in the Excelsiors lineup, pitching as normal.

Creighton played with the Excelsiors until late September of 1862, when there was a second round of rumors. On September 26th the *Daily Eagle* reported that Creighton, Flanley and Asa Brainard had joined the Atlantics. *Wilkes' Spirit of the Times* reported the same on October 4th. On October 8th the Brooklyn *Times Union* also printed the news that Creighton, Brainard and Flanley had left the Excelsiors for the Atlantics. On September 26th the Excelsiors played the Stars. George Flanley pitched. Creighton was absent without explanation, as was Asa Brainard. Even more intriguing, the Brooklyn *Daily Eagle* of October 6 reports the following:

> The Excelsiors have now become to be regarded as a half-dead club...The match on Saturday was an impromptu affair...both clubs were short-handed—the Excelsiors' three first-nine men, Russell, Thompson and Young being absent.

Three weeks later, James Creighton was back with the Excelsiors, playing his final, fatal game against the Unions.

Why did the *Daily Eagle* not mention that James Creighton was missing from the Excelsiors' lineup on September 26, while reporting the absence of other starting players? The obvious answer is that they knew that Creighton was no longer a member of the Excelsiors. This explains much more than why Creighton missed one game in September of 1862. Consider the following scenario. Going all the way back to the beginning of 1858, the Excelsiors supported James Creighton, Jr. and his family. In 1860, the Excelsiors paid Creighton a good salary via not one, but two no-show jobs at the Custom House. When baseball stopped after the outbreak of the Civil War in 1861, the support stopped. Whatever Creighton may have been paid for playing cricket in 1861, it was likely not enough. In the spring of 1862 James Creighton, Jr. needed money. He threatened to leave the club for the Atlantics, who had made it known that they intended to be more active than the Excelsiors that season. The Atlantics were less orthodox about amateurism than the Excelsiors; they supported their players with sinecures and cushy government jobs thanks to their sponsorship by Brooklyn's Democratic political machine. The embarrassment to baseball of its biggest star openly following the money to another club was avoided when Creighton was convinced to stay, no doubt by payment of some kind. In late 1862 the Excelsiors had either not delivered on whatever assurances they had made to Creighton in the spring, or Creighton simply needed more money for his father, his brother or himself. He jumped to the Atlantics for real in September, but the baseball powers-that-were intervened, paid Creighton to go back, and then denied that any of it had ever happened, to protect amateur baseball's public image.

There is corroborating evidence for this scenario. Sometime in late 1862 or early 1863, but no later than March 1863, James Creighton, Sr. came into possession of another house. This one was the same size as 307 Henry Street, his home since 1858. It was located literally next door at 309 Henry. The seller is listed on the Land Conveyance record as John Morrison. Builder John Morrison is the same man who was listed five years earlier as the seller of 307 Henry Street. As it had in 1858, the club appears to have been paying James Creighton, Jr. not in cash, which would have been too stark a violation of amateur baseball's rules and culture, but in real estate. After October 18th, 1862, the Creighton household consisted of two people, James Creighton, Sr. and his unmarried daughter Mary Ann. They had no need of another house. Houses, however, can be sold or rented out. It is not hard to understand why this transaction would have gone through even after James Jr.'s death. The club still owed him and his family.

This puts the circumstances of James Creighton, Jr.'s final game on October 14th in a different light. We now know that he was suffering from a chronic physical condition that was worsening. He was wearing down and in obvious pain during the St. George-Willow Club match of October 7, 1862. We also know that he was too ill to start the October 14 Unions game as pitcher, and that despite this he played and even made an emergency relief appearance. Remembering Creighton's death in 1887, Henry Chadwick wrote:

> I saw Creighton play in a cricket match at Bedford, on the outskirts of Brooklyn, as a member of the St. George Club, in a game with the Willow Club eleven in 1862, and in that match, in making a very hard effort to hit a leg ball, Creighton unknowingly ruptured himself. Not aware of the serious injury he sustained on the occasion, he very un-prudently engaged in a baseball match with the Excelsiors, of Brooklyn, against the Unions, of Morrisania, and he had not pitched long in the game before he had to retire from his position from pain.

Chadwick's use of the word "un-prudently" here is suggestive. Once again, consider the timing. In the spring of 1862 James Creighton threatens to quit the Excelsiors unless they help him. In September he repeats his demand or asks for more. Not satisfied, he then jumps to the Excelsiors' archrivals, the Atlantics. The Excelsiors promise him a valuable piece of real estate if he returns. Creighton agrees, but his hernia is worsening. He continues to play cricket, a sport with no prohibition against paying top players in cash, perhaps $10 or $20 per game. He is in pain, but instead of resting he takes the money and plays for the St. George cricket club on October 7th. As the Excelsiors' game against the Unions approaches, Creighton is in a difficult position. After pressuring the Excelsiors (twice) to help him financially, and after playing cricket on October 7th, how could he refuse to play for the Excelsiors against the Unions on October 14th?

There is no way to know if skipping the cricket match or the October 14 baseball game in 1862 might have saved or extended James Creighton's life. But we do know what he did. He did what professional pitchers do—play hurt.

Every baseball season from 1857 to 1868 began with the question: can anyone beat the Atlantics? At center in plain clothes is Atlantics captain Pete O'Brien, who faced Creighton as a batter and umpired games in which Creighton pitched.

5 The Three Kings

In 1860 all of the best baseball clubs in America played in Brooklyn. Twentieth-century baseball had stretches of time when more than one New York team won pennants, but nothing like Brooklyn's dominance in the Amateur Era, when a triumvirate of great clubs — the Atlantics, Eckfords and Excelsiors — reigned over the sport. One of these three won every national baseball championship for a nine-year period.

The Eckfords won back-to-back championships in the Civil War years of 1862 and 1863. The championship series of 1860 between the Atlantics and Excelsiors was disputed, and there was no real baseball season in 1861. But the Atlantics won in 1857, 1858, 1859, 1864, 1865 and 1866. They were the Amateur Era's answer to the New York Yankees of Mantle, Berra and Ford. The fact that the national baseball championship was an exclusively Brooklyn affair did not dampen national interest. On the contrary, as Americans everywhere picked up bats and balls and started their own clubs in the 1860s, they followed the battles and rivalries of the Brooklyn baseball kings through the press. Some called baseball "the Brooklyn game." Big crowds turned out and vast sums were wagered when one of the Brooklyn big three came to town. Clubs from Baltimore to Chicago to Albany took the names Atlantic, Eckford or Excelsior. They even named themselves after famous Brooklyn players. There was a Joe Leggett Club in upstate New York. A search through nineteenth-century American newspapers (the minority that have been digitized) found baseball clubs named after James Creighton in Norfolk, Virginia; Piermont, New York; Mount Vernon, New York; and Washington, DC. There were certainly many more.

How good were the Atlantics? Historians tend to punt on this question on the grounds that the numbers from the Amateur Era are next to useless. They have a point. Run totals were so high that they leave modern fans scratching their heads. Part of the reason is that before Creighton pitching was underhand and slow, like some types of modern softball. Another is that fields were nothing like today's manicured putting greens, and fielders played without gloves. That included the catcher, who was a human backstop; his main responsibility was to block pitches without the aid of a mitt, shin guards, padding or a facemask. At that time passed balls and wild pitches were shockingly common, and they often decided the outcome of a game. The 1860 Atlantics scored in double figures in 13 of their 14 full-length games; they scored 20 or more runs in a third of their games. When the 1860 Brooklyn Excelsiors demolished the Baltimore Excelsiors by the football score of 51–9, Baltimore reporters did not complain that their team had been shown up; they thought that the Brooklynites had held down the score to be good sports. The 1860 Unions' 7–4 defeat of the Excelsiors made headlines—because only 11 men crossed the plate. It was called "one of the smallest scores on record." With no fixed schedule or organized leagues, clubs played opponents of wildly varying quality, so seasonal winning percentages mean little or nothing. A 10–3 club could be inferior to a 5–9 club and often was. Lineups varied from year to year, even from game to game; players sometimes switched positions out of whimsy; and not all games were taken equally seriously by the participants.

There are other places to look for answers, however, than in the box scores. The career trajectories of individual players show us that Brooklyn's baseball dominance far outlasted the greatness of its great Amateur Era clubs. Even though the Atlantics' heyday came in the Amateur Era, a significant number of their players went on to have long careers in pro baseball, which began with the National Association in 1871. (Major League Baseball, at least as Major League Baseball defines it, began in 1876, the first year of the National League). Brooklyn clubs were not generally successful in the early professional era, but the city remained the sport's go-to source of talent. When clubs from

Cleveland to Chicago to Washington, DC needed a pitcher or a second baseman, they went shopping in Brooklyn. Ex-Atlantic players are all over the founding and development of professional baseball, as players but also as managers, scouts, executives and officials. Outfielder Jack Chapman played through 1876 and then managed six major and minor-league clubs, the last in 1892. Catcher Bob Ferguson played professionally through 1884, served as president of the professional National Association, managed until 1887 and umpired 786 major-league games. Lipman Pike won a National League home run title and retired as a professional player in 1887 when he was 42. Dickey Pearce played shortstop in the major leagues at 41 years old and first baseman Joe Start played regularly until 1886, when he was 43. These numbers are trying to tell us something. If we started seeing, say, dozens of 40-something players coming from Japan to today's MLB and winning starting jobs, we might begin to question the competitive superiority of Major League Baseball.

The Atlantics were also unique in their relationship with the citizens of Brooklyn. The essence of modern professional baseball's appeal as entertainment is fan identification. A fan is essentially a spectator who commits emotionally to a team. As relationships go, this one is a one-way street. Modern fans whose regular position is center recliner say "we" won, or "we" lost, when the actual winners are a collection of hired strangers. Fandom and sports are inseparable today, but this was not always true. Early Amateur Era clubs played for and represented only themselves. Hardly anyone cared enough to watch. In the 1840s and early 1850s crowds in the hundreds were a cause for wonderment or — if the crowd was made up of gamblers and bookmakers — dismay. New Yorkers who took the ferry to Hoboken might have stopped to watch the Knickerbockers or the Eagles play baseball; some might have had a bet down on the game, but they did not have a fan's rooting interest. The first fans appeared in late 1850s Brooklyn. They were rooting for clubs that came from their own neighborhood; they were Eckford fans or Excelsior fans or Atlantic fans. By the 1860s, however, the Atlantics had become Brooklyn's team — the first baseball club to truly represent a city. As we will see, Brooklyn fans overwhelmingly favored the Atlantics in their 1860 championship series against the Excelsiors, and this played a role in the outcome. The relationship between Brooklyn and the Atlantics was so strong that it outlived both amateur baseball and the Atlantic Club itself. The reason why lies in how Brooklyn itself happened.

In 1820, the word *Brooklyn* meant a town of fewer than 12,000 people that had grown up around the ferry that linked Long Island to lower Manhattan. If you could visit in a time machine, you might think you were in a New England fishing village. Most of its inhabitants made their living in some way from the water. An 1815 map of Brooklyn shows the stalls of fish dealers, butchers and grocers near Fulton Ferry who supplied New York City's Fly Market, which was located where Maiden Lane meets the East River. Brooklynites also worked in the warehouses, ships and boats that served New York Harbor, the receiving point for most of what America imported from the rest of the world. The Atlantic baseball club had its roots in this Brooklyn. This was the Brooklyn that poet and journalist Walt Whitman cherished, and that the Brooklyn Bridge, mass transportation and highways later wiped out. In Whitman's poem "Crossing Brooklyn Ferry," the ferry embodies Brooklyn's defining connection to the water, and the river it crosses keeps two very different cities apart:

> Flow on, river! flow with the flood-tide, and ebb with the ebb-tide!
> Frolic on, crested and scallop-edg'd waves!
> Gorgeous clouds of the sunset! drench with your splendor me, or the men and women generations after me!
> Cross from shore to shore, countless crowds of passengers!
> Stand up, tall masts of Mannahatta! stand up, beautiful hills of Brooklyn!

Mid-nineteenth-century New York City was growing fast, but Whitman's Brooklyn was growing even faster, doubling its population each decade and reaching over 800,000 by 1890. Brooklyn also expanded geographically. In 1855, just as the sport of baseball was taking off, Brooklyn annexed both the city of Williamsburg and the town of Bushwick, which included Greenpoint, where the Eckford Club was founded that same year. Like Brooklyn Heights, Williamsburg began as an upscale suburb populated by well-to-do Manhattanites. The Putnam club was founded there in 1855.

Baseball came to bucolic Greenpoint with the shipbuilding industry, which in the 1840s and 1850s was gradually relocating from Manhattan to the other side of the East River. Williamsburg, Bushwick and Greenpoint were initially known as the "Eastern District," and they retained an identity apart from the rest of Brooklyn until quite recently. (There was an Eastern District Railroad terminal until 1983 and an Eastern District High School until 1996).

A map of Brooklyn made before the additions of 1855 would extend from Wallabout Bay to Red Hook, with the ferry district in the middle. In 1801 the US government bought 40 acres on Wallabout Bay to establish the Brooklyn Navy Yard and build naval vessels. Shipbuilding boomed during the War of 1812 and the yard imported skilled labor from Great Britain, including a smattering of Irish Catholics who had worked in the shipyards of Derry in Ulster. Most of them were, like James Creighton, Sr., natives of County Donegal, which borders Derry. In 1822, leaders of Brooklyn's small Irish Catholic community met to create a parish and raise funds for Brooklyn's first Catholic church, St. James. At that meeting were several Irish-born men whose surnames who would become important in the history of Irish America, New York — and baseball. One was Patrick McCloskey, whose son John became the second archbishop of New York and the first president of Fordham College, a baseball factory that provided talent to the Union Club of Morrisania and, later, professional clubs. Fordham also produced Esteban Bellan, the founding father of Cuban baseball. Another was James Furey, a refugee from the Irish Rebellion of 1798 and father of politician Robert Furey, who cofounded the Pastimes, a club made up of Brooklyn politicians and civil servants; and Hugh McLaughlin, whose son of the same name built the greatest Irish political organization in American history. Hugh McLaughlin, Jr. and Robert Furey were childhood friends, co-workers in the Navy Yard and political partners. McLaughlin did not play baseball above the sandlot level, but the Pastime baseball club was full of lieutenants in his political machine, and he used the power and resources of Brooklyn City Hall to support the Atlantic Club. For the McLaughlin machine, baseball was a pastime and an amenity for its constituents. It was also a political resource. The pride that rank-and-file Brooklynites took in the success of the Atlantic Club cemented their loyalty to the party bosses who sponsored it.

Brooklyn's first Irish Catholics lived along the East River in the neighborhoods of Vinegar Hill (named after the decisive battle in the 1798 Irish Rebellion), Irishtown (also called "The Forty Acres") and the ferry district. After serving his adopted country by digging trenches and building fortifications during the War of 1812, Donegal-born Hugh McLaughlin, Sr. opened a grocery store on Everitt Street, a few steps from the Brooklyn Ferry landing. In 1815, near the present Cadman Plaza, he built the White House tavern, which served as a gathering place for Democratic politicians for 75 years. Hugh, Jr. was born on Everitt Street in 1827. He worked as a boy for a ropemaker before partnering with his brother, on a lighter, a flat-bottomed barge used for moving goods to and from moored ships.

In the late 1840s and 1850s, Hugh McLaughlin, Jr. entered politics and began to rise in the hierarchy of the Brooklyn Democratic Party, then controlled by old money landowners and merchants. He still needed a day job. In the 1857 Brooklyn City Directory he is listed as a fish dealer in the Atlantic Market. Both market traders and politicians were baseball enthusiasts. A look through the Brooklyn Democratic leadership in 1857 turns up baseball men including John McNamee and Frank Quevedo of the Pastime Club, and Henry Manolt of the Eckfords. It also includes Hugh McLaughlin, Jr., who had leveraged his relationships in the Irish Catholic community, the waterfront and the Atlantic Market to become Brooklyn's Democratic Party leader. After he helped get George Taylor elected to Congress in 1857, he was rewarded with a federal patronage job, the position of master or boss laborer at the Brooklyn Navy Yard. This gave him control over high-paying federal jobs, which in turn gained him more friends and allies. During the Civil War military spending skyrocketed and McLaughlin was able to employ a small army of Irish immigrants who were loyal to him personally.

McLaughlin's rise in politics was timed perfectly to benefit from the Potato Famine immigration, which turned Brooklyn, as well as New York, into a kind of West Ireland. In 1855—ten years after the arrival of the first famine refugees—one fourth of Brooklyn's population was born in Ireland. McLaughlin was called "Boss" (like "stoop," "cookie" and "bedspread," the word "boss' entered New York vernacular from Dutch) not because of his political power but because of his Navy Yard position. In fact, the word acquired its present political connotation because of its association with McLaughlin, not the other way around. The notorious political boss William Tweed of New York City was named "Boss" after Hugh McLaughlin. In 1861 McLaughlin was elected Kings County Register, whatever that was. He remained in this low-profile job for decades, preferring to play cards in the back room of an auction house on Willoughby Street, quietly issuing orders and pulling strings. He picked every Democratic candidate for every office and controlled Brooklyn and its Democratic party, with minor interruptions, from 1857 to 1904. McLaughlin's common touch and dry sense of humor helped him navigate periodic scandals. (When he was accused of tipping off friendly real estate developers about where a new subway line was going to be built, his defense was to say that *someone's* friends were going to get rich from owning land near the subway—why not his?) McLaughlin was also a good Catholic boy; he was comfortable with some categories of sin, but he detested Tammany Hall, the vice-friendly Democratic Party organization across the river, for what he called its "red-light politics." But Hugh McLaughlin's greatest political asset was his grayness. For most of his career, few non-political insiders knew exactly what he did or how he did it.

The idea of organized baseball clubs on the Knickerbocker model arrived in Brooklyn in the mid-1850s, but the game of baseball had beat them to it. The butchers, fish dealers, grocers and dairymen of the Atlantic Market, which was located on the Brooklyn waterfront, played once a week after work. When they decided to form a club, they merged with the better players from another pickup game that included the Babcock brothers, who were engravers with connections to New York City's Empire baseball club; this game also begat the Pastime Club. It was located on an open lot near the intersection of York and Jay Streets, around the corner from Hugh McLaughlin, Sr.'s White House tavern and not far from Mike Henry's bar, which later served as the Atlantics' headquarters.

High atop Brooklyn Heights was another vacant lot, bounded by Sidney Place. Its eccentric owner kept it undeveloped while the rest of the neighborhood was being subdivided into 25' x 100' building lots, following the grid plan created by suburban visionary Hezekiah Pierrepont. A boys' afternoon pickup baseball game sprung up on Sydney Place and ultimately begat the Star, Excelsior, Charter Oak and other South Brooklyn clubs. Fulton Street, originally part of an ancient Native American footpath that led from the East River all the way to Montauk, was the dividing line between Brooklyn proper and Brooklyn Heights. In precolonial days smaller footpaths branched off from the main path and led to the top of the Heights and its panoramic view of Manhattan and New York Bay. One of these one of became Grace Court Alley and another Love Lane. Both survive today, wantonly ignoring Pierrepont's grid.

These two Brooklyn pickup games were separated by attitude as well as altitude. The Atlantics and Pastimes belonged to the old waterfront and ferry Brooklyn. They were the children of boatmen, sailmakers, ropemakers, butchers and grocers. The Excelsiors and Stars were from new Brooklyn, the commuter suburb that had sprung up on Brooklyn Heights after New York and Brooklyn were linked by daily steam ferry service in 1814. They lived in brownstones and rowhouses like the one on Henry Street that the Creightons moved into in 1858 and where James Creighton, Jr. died. Most of them were the children of merchants, bankers, stockbrokers and professionals, who commuted to downtown Manhattan.

The communities that these games grew out of were natural rivals. As far back as the 1820s, Brooklyn youth gangs with names like the "40 Acres," "Roosters," and "Rocks" had regular fights with each other in the street. Their battles were about turf, but in a larger sense they were about the comfortable versus the working class, American-born versus immigrant, democratic versus aristocratic, and the heights versus the flats. When the boys in these gangs grew older, they joined the volunteer fire department, bringing with them their class identities and their antagonisms. Before 1865, when the fire departments of New York and Brooklyn were professionalized, volunteer fire companies were self-constituted grassroots organizations. They performed a necessary public service, but there was also a competitive element to what was called "running with the machine." Companies raced each other to get to a fire first, often with help of young would-be firemen who would direct traffic, help pull engines and sabotage or block rival companies' equipment. It was not unknown for two volunteer fire houses to settle their differences with fists while the fire they were fighting over blazed away. Friendly fire companies also paid elaborate visits to each other, where they held banquets and entertained the public with competitions of firefighting skills. If this sounds like the behavior of early Amateur Era baseball clubs, it is because baseball clubs and firehouses were commonly made up of people who were very similar—or the same. It was not unusual for a baseball club and a fire company to have overlapping membership. Both might also overlap with the roster of citizen militia units, which were also community-based volunteer organizations. Baseball imported elements of firefighting culture, from ritual exchanges of hospitality to uniforms modeled on those worn by firemen.

Founding and early members of the Atlantic baseball club belonged to volunteer fire companies located near the waterfront and the ferry district: Constitution Engine #7, the heroes of Irishtown; Mechanics Hose #2; Washington Hose #1; and Atlantic Hose #1. Early Atlantics players Daniel Brayton, Stephen Mann and Harvey Ross were important members of Mechanics Hose #2. All were sailmakers; Brayton worked at the Brooklyn Navy Yard, where Hugh McLaughlin was the man to see if you wanted work. Mechanics Hose #2's nickname, the "Roosters," hints at a link to the street gang of that name. Hugh McLaughlin himself belonged to Washington Hose #1.

Members of these companies looked at Pacific Engine #14, located on Love Lane in Brooklyn Heights, in the same way that the children of the working waterfront viewed the rich kids from the Heights. Pacific Engine #14 was the fire company most closely associated with the Excelsiors. In the early 1860s, when everyone in Brooklyn was forming baseball clubs, volunteer fire companies fielded their own teams and pursued their rivalries on the baseball field. Atlantic Hose #1, for example played baseball games against Pacific Engine #14, often on the Atlantics' or the Excelsiors' home grounds. A history of the Brooklyn Fire Department notes that Pacific Engine #14 was known as the "dude Company of the Heights" for its smartly dressed and socially ambitious members. It was "one of the conspicuous companies of the old department...both in fire duty and in personal influence." Similarly, the Excelsiors' parent club, the Knickerbockers, had one foot in Oceana Hose #36 in Manhattan, a company that was known for its style and superfine banquets; it was nicknamed the "Quills" because so many of its members clerked in Wall Street offices. Before he became the Excelsiors' catcher, Joe Leggett served as foreman of Pacific #14, as did his brother and a cousin. When the Excelsiors were dormant in the early Civil War years, Leggett and teammates George Flanley and Harry Polhemus appear in lineups for the Pacific #14 team against the Atlantic Hose #1 team.

The Atlantic Market, founded in 1847 at the corner of Atlantic Avenue and Hicks Street, gave birth to the Atlantic baseball club in 1855. The club's political godfather, Hugh McLaughlin, Jr., worked there. A long list of early Atlantics players were grocers, fish dealers, butchers or dairymen. Club founders include butcher Caleb Sniffen, and butter and cheese dealer Thomas Tassie. Brothers Mattie and

Peter O'Brien, the heart of the early Atlantics dynasty, originally sold butter. Slugging first baseman Joe Start's father was an Atlantic market fish dealer.

The Atlantics were almost as aggressive about developing talent as the Excelsiors, their rivals on the Heights. Future star shortstop Dickey Pearce joined the club in 1856; he was born in Brooklyn, but his only connection to the Atlantic market traders was that they liked the way he played shortstop. The Atlantics caused a scandal by poaching several players from the Harmony Club. They acquired prospects from junior organizations such as the Enterprise Club. Like the Excelsiors, the Atlantics found ways to support their key players that skirted the rule against player compensation. Thanks to the patronage of Hugh McLaughlin, Atlantics players were given sinecures, no-show jobs or city contracts during and after their playing days. Atlantics captain and former market trader Pete O'Brien owned a construction business that depended on business with the city. Shortstop Pearce worked—or was paid to work—for the Brooklyn Water Board. The Babcock brothers got city printing jobs. Steve Mann was a Brooklyn fire warden. In retirement pitcher George Zettlein was hired as a clerk in Brooklyn City Hall. As Henry Chadwick later put it, "In those days, the ball tossers...were well taken care of by the politicians. [Atlantics third baseman Charlie] Smith occupied a berth under [City] Register Billy Barre." Barre was a Hugh McLaughlin associate and a member of the Pastime baseball club.

The Atlantics' historic run of championships began in Bedford, where the club made its first home baseball grounds. Better known today as the inner-city neighborhood of Bedford-Stuyvesant, Bedford was then a country village whose hotels and resorts attracted an English expat clientele. They offered English beer, mutton chops and English sports such as quoits, lawn bowling and cricket. Bedford was reachable from downtown Brooklyn via the Fulton Street stagecoach line operated by Charles Holder, an Englishman who owned Bedford's Three-Mile House, called that because it was exactly three miles from the Fulton Ferry landing.

The Excelsiors spent their early years playing catch-up with the Atlantics. The Excelsiors played no games against other clubs in 1855 and only two in 1856, both against the socially compatible Putnams. The Atlantics won seven games with a loss and a tie in 1857. That year the Excelsiors played only three games against other clubs, splitting a pair with the Unions and losing to the Putnams. Eighteen-fifty-seven was also the year the Excelsiors merged with the Wayne Club and acquired both catcher Joe Leggett and star outfielder John Holder, the English hotel-keeper's American son. The Excelsiors felt good about their chances as they entered the 1858 season; they had an improved lineup and energetic club leadership. Another reason for optimism was playing for the Niagaras — the young prospect James Creighton.

In the spring of 1858, the Excelsiors' dreams of parity with the Atlantics collided with reality. The presidents of the Brooklyn clubs felt ready to show the world that that they had surpassed New York City in baseball. They issued a challenge to their counterparts across the river: a best-two-of-three series between two teams made up of

Amateur Baseball created America's first real fans. Spectators were not invited to the party, but they crashed it, showing up by the hundreds and thousands to games in the late 1850s, standing in foul territory and rooting for their favorite players.

the best players from each city. New York City accepted. These were the first baseball games that anyone ever paid to see. General admission was ten cents.

Modern sports fans spend tremendous amounts of time and money on professional sports. On most summer nights, a dozen or more major-league baseball stadiums across the country sell thirty, forty or fifty thousand tickets. Smaller crowds attend hundreds of minor league and college games. Millions watch baseball on TV. And baseball is only one of our several national professional sports. Before 1858 there might have been the odd crowd as high as several thousand at a prize fight, horse race or political rally, but not at a ballgame — or any team sport. The big game, especially an inter-city matchup, was unexplored sporting territory. Everything about the Fashion Course Series was new and unprecedented. Before the opening game, New York announced that it would pick its players from only the Knickerbockers, Eagles, Empires and Gothams, setting off cries of favoritism by the many clubs who were excluded. Brooklyn also played politics, allocating slots in the Brooklyn lineup by club affiliation, not by any baseball criteria. The first two batters, Leggett and Holder, were Excelsiors, followed by two Eckfords, Pidgeon and Grum. Then came three Atlantics, Pete O'Brien, Price and Mattie O'Brien; and, finally, two Putnams, Masten and Burr. As a member of a youth club, James Creighton was too young to be considered.

The pregame and early betting line heavily favored Brooklyn, but the odds reversed in the fourth and fifth inning, when Atlantics pitcher Mattie O'Brien gave up 11 runs. The final was a 22–18 upset victory for New York. Facing elimination, Brooklyn tightened things up. They put together a game two lineup of five Atlantics, three Eckfords, one Putnam — and zero Excelsiors. Pitcher Frank Pidgeon of the Eckfords beat New York, 29–8. The Excelsiors were livid about being excluded. The *Sunday Mercury* reported that "It was expected that Holder and Leggett, of the Excelsior Club, would play in the Brooklyn nine: but a misunderstanding occurred, which led to their withdrawal." The Excelsiors blamed the "misunderstanding" on the Eckfords, and they held a grudge; the two clubs did not play each other for nine years.

In the deciding game three, Brooklyn was represented by only two clubs—six Atlantics and three Eckfords. The Putnams joined the Excelsiors on the bench. New York won the game, 29–18, and the series. Regardless of the outcome, it is hard to second-guess Brooklyn's personnel changes in games two and three. The Putnams had one or two good players, but they were not in the same class as the Atlantics, and they knew it. Neither were the Excelsiors, who went into the offseason angry and more determined than ever to find a way to beat the Atlantics. This is the same offseason in which James Creighton was converted from an infielder to a pitcher.

At the time of the Fashion Course Series, both Creighton and talented position player George Flanley were playing for the Niagaras, the lesser of the two junior clubs affiliated with the Excelsiors. John Shields was the Niagaras' everyday pitcher; Creighton played exclusively in the infield, at second or third base. He had a good reputation as a hitter and as a fielder, but both improved in the decades after he died. Reference sources today still repeat the crazy lie that he once went an entire season without making a single out. How good a position player was he, really?

Judging Creighton as a hitter is difficult because of poor recordkeeping. Great minds work wonders with modern baseball statistics, but the numbers from Creighton's day are maddeningly crude. Box scores from 1860, for example, tell us the position where a player started the game, but they often do not say if or when he was moved to another position or taken out of a game. They tell us how many runs a hitter scored, which is valuable, and "hands lost" (or "hands out"), which is not. If a "hand lost" meant that the batter had made an out, then we would have something to work with. We could calculate runs scored per out for individual hitters, which is not a useless statistic. Unfortunately, however, the way they did it then was that a batter turned baserunner was given a hand lost if he was tagged out, forced out or put out in any way—at any time during the inning. In other words, if Creighton singled four times in four at-bats in a game but was forced at second each time by another Excelsior batter, his line in the box score would look like this: 0 runs, 4 hands lost. If he came up four times and hit four singles and scored four runs, then his line would look like this: 4 runs, 0 hands lost. The way we look at it today, he went four-for-four in both games.

None of Creighton's contemporaries thought he was as good a hitter as he was a pitcher. Still, he was very good. If we look at runs scored per game, he ranks high, but not as high as Joe Leggett and one or two other teammates. According to an 1866 story in the Brooklyn *Daily Eagle*, the Excelsiors kept a silver ball in their clubhouse on which they inscribed the name of each season's best hitter. This was based on batting statistics, but we do not know if they included intramural games, some inter-club games or all games. In 1860 it was Joseph Leggett. The Excelsiors played very few games against other clubs in 1861 and 1862, but for those years the name on the silver ball was James Creighton.

People who saw Creighton play thought that he was an excellent fielder, but the best infielders of Creighton's day played shortstop or catcher. Creighton never played either position. He played third base at the beginning of his career and later switched to second base. Obviously, he had a strong arm, which raises the question of why he was playing second, which in modern baseball is a position where defensive range, agility—and, of course, a good bat—are more important than arm strength. Today, a good defensive infielder with a powerful arm usually plays shortstop or, if he has power and quickness but lacks range, at third. During the late Amateur Era, however, the shortstop position was evolving from a universal cutoff man for throws from the outfield into an extra infielder. In 1859 that evolution was not entirely complete. In the 1860 edition of the instructional *Beadle's Dime Base Ball Player*, Henry Chadwick says this about playing second base:

> This position is considered by many to be the key of the field, and therefore requires an excellent player to occupy it. He should be an accurate and swift thrower, a sure catcher and a thorough fielder. He should play a little back of his base, and to the left or right of it, according to the habitual play of the striker [batter], but generally to the left, as most balls pass in that direction.

Apparently the second basemen of that time were expected to cover more ground than their modern counterparts. Most intriguing of all, Amateur Era second basemen routinely over-shifted, often playing on the left field side of the infield, in the same way and for the same reason as major league clubs did until 2023, when MLB introduced a rule limiting the practice.

The box scores from Creighton's games are not much help in judging Creighton's defense, with two exceptions. One is from the Niagaras' August 31, 1858, game against the Phoenix club. That day the Niagaras were short-handed and played only eight men in the field. They put Creighton at third and did not use a shortstop, so Creighton was in effect manning the entire left side of the infield. The Niagaras won the game, 23–22. The other is from the Excelsiors' 1860 visit to Baltimore. In the late innings of that game, Creighton switched places with left fielder Ed Russell. With two men on, according to the Sunday Mercury, "By one of the handsomest backward single-handed catches ever made by Creighton, he took the ball on the fly, and instantly, by a true and rapid throw, passed the ball to Whiting, who caught it, and threw it as quickly to Brainard on the second base, before either [runner] had time to return to their bases, thus putting three hands out 'in a jiffy.'.... This entire performance was so quickly and neatly done that it elicited a spontaneous mark of approbation and applause from the vast assemblage of spectators..." This is one of the earliest known triple plays.

Eighteen-year-old James Creighton threw his first pitch that counted in midsummer of 1859 for the Niagaras. Like a real-life Sidd Finch, off the field Creighton had been working on an experimental new pitching style. But rumors of an amazing breakthrough were leaking out. The reveal took place on July 19th. We know from other sources that left-handed slow pitcher Shields started this game for the Niagaras and that James Creighton came on in relief in the fifth inning, with the Niagaras behind by several runs. Based on the published box scores, Creighton held down the Stars' hitters for a couple of innings, before he (or possibly someone else, who knows?) allowed two runs in the seventh and three more in the eighth. The game stories and the box scores in the

Sunday Mercury, the *New York Times* and the *New York Clipper* all fail to mention the unusual fact that Shields was replaced—starters in that era typically went the whole game—or that the man who replaced him, James Creighton, was making his widely anticipated first appearance as a pitcher. Today, that would have been the headline. None of the reporters seemed to have realized that the baseball insiders who came to this game *knew in advance* that Creighton would be pitching. That is why they were there. The *Times* reported that "an unusually large audience, numbering representations from almost every New York and Brooklyn club, were gratified spectators of this well-contested game," but did not bother to wonder why.

What they saw was a new kind of pitching that was, in Atlantics star Jack Chapman's words, "fairly unhittable." A skinny, long-limbed teenager had come to rewrite the rulebook and turn baseball inside out. Creighton had astonishing velocity, but there was more to it than that; his pitches veered, darted and broke, but always with perfect control and always with purpose. We have later eyewitness accounts from some of those spectators, including writer Henry Chadwick and Atlantics player Pete O'Brien. Writing about this game in *The Ball Player's Chronicle* in 1869, Chadwick said that the Stars "soon saw that they could not cope with such pitching." Completely overwhelmed, the Stars fell back on a tactic that later opponents would resort to repeatedly when they faced Creighton. They put in a pitcher who threw hard, but whose pitches were too wild to for batters to reach. This turned the game into a tedious waiting contest. James Creighton was unhittable, but for an entirely different reason. "When Creighton got to work," O'Brien recalled, "we saw something new in [base]ball."

It was new to them, but not to us. What they saw was pitching.

A Currier and Ives depiction of an imaginary game between the c. 1860 Atlantics and Excelsiors. James Creighton is pitching. Note the second baseman playing straight up the middle and the gloveless, unmasked and unpadded catcher standing close to the plate.

6 A FAIR AND SQUARE PITCH

I ONCE RAN INTO former major-league pitcher Tom Browning in a bar in Hamilton, Ohio. We got into a conversation about the history of pitching. I showed him what the pitcher's delivery looked like before Creighton came along. Then I asked him how hard he believed he could throw like that. He thought about it and said, "40–50 mph max." That is probably in the ballpark.

Velocity is the biggest difference between pitching today and pitching before Creighton. Modern baseball rules make no attempt to limit how hard pitchers can throw. Today we live in a brave new world of 100 mph fastballs and 90 mph changeups. Of course, velocity is not the only difference. Today's pitchers can hold, grip and spin the ball any way they like. They can deceive batters with changing arm angles, varying release points and—sadly for me and millions of other former 12-year-olds who dreamed of playing in the big leagues—pitches that curve. The Amateur Era rules required that Creighton deliver the ball dead underhand, and the ball had to be pitched, not thrown. In modern baseball these two words are often interchangeable. Pitchers throw and throwers pitch. This is confusing unless you know that the original meaning of "pitching" was using a straight-arm underhand motion like that used in playing horseshoes. "Throwing" meant pronating the forearm to turn the ball outward and jerking an arm bent at the elbow straight, to achieve a whip-like action. Pronating the forearm allows the pitcher to snap his wrist using the joint's greatest range of motion. This is less complicated than it sounds. What James Creighton's rulebook called throwing is what almost everybody who throws a baseball does today, whether they are throwing underhand or overhand. But when Creighton was alive, if you were a pitcher, throwing was cheating.

In the Amateur Era, the rules governing pitching deliveries changed over time, but their purpose remained the same: to handicap the pitcher. Early baseball was a battle of hitting versus fielding, not hitting versus pitching. The idea was that hitters would get pitches to hit; they would hit them hard; and the winning team would be the one whose defense turned more hard-hit balls into outs. (This is how many forms of modern softball work). To make it even worse for pitchers, in the 1850s and 1860s the baseball was bigger and much more elastic than today's ball. In modern baseball parlance, the pitchers chucked and ducked. After that, the game was literally in the hands of the fielders.

To Doc Adams of the old Knickerbockers, longtime chairman of amateur baseball's rules committee, this was how baseball was supposed to be. In an 1896 interview, he complained: "The pitcher... [formerly] pitched the ball so the batsman could strike it and give some work to the fielders... Nowadays the game seems to be played almost entirely by the pitcher and catcher." Before Creighton, the batters and the fielders were main characters, and the pitcher played a supporting role. In earlier, primitive forms of baseball, the pitcher was even less important than that; he was a mere stagehand, feeding the ball gently to the batter so that he could put it in play and the action could begin. This underlies the vestigial language in the old baseball rules that says that pitchers must throw the ball "to the bat." When James Creighton made his pitching debut in 1859, this rule was not yet dead letter, but it was in failing health. Because the umpire did not call balls or strikes, there was no penalty for pitchers who could not or would not throw to the bat; nor was there a penalty for batters who refused to swing at hittable pitches. Until James Creighton came along, pitchers and hitters had cooperated anyway because not doing so made the game pointless.

The increasing competition of the 1850s pressured pitchers to come up with ways to prevent batters from barreling up the baseball. They did their best with what little they had to work with. There was no pitcher's plate or rubber; pitchers were allowed to run up to a line.

Think of cricket bowling, but underhand and without the ball touching the ground. But because the pitching line was 12 feet long, pitchers could come at batters from different angles. It also helped that the line was only 45 feet from home plate—versus today's 60 feet, six inches from the pitcher's plate to home—but this advantage counted for little when pitchers were throwing as slow as they did before Creighton. Post-Creighton sports journalism is full of talk about the good old days when "medium" or "slow-paced" pitchers used "head work"—a favorite phrase of Henry Chadwick—to fool batters into making less than optimal contact. They changed speeds from slow to slower and back again. They were supposed to pitch "to the bat," but if they had good enough control, they could do so while keeping the ball away from the batter's happy zone.

The best slow pitchers were famed for their skill in pitching to their defense, for example, by preventing batters from pulling the ball or by forcing them do so. As Chadwick wrote in 1884: "[Eckfords pitcher] Frank Pidgeon...was a practical exemplar of the old-time strategic method of pitching the ball to the bat, which was in vogue before Creighton inaugurated the swift underhand throwing [*sic*] to the bat; a method [that is, pitching slowly to the bat] in which Matty O'Brien of the Atlantics; Tom Dakin of the Putnams; and Ed Russell of the Excelsiors were noted exponents." Strikeouts were extremely rare for obvious reasons. Even the wiliest slow pitchers and the headiest head workers were fatally dependent on fielders who played without gloves on rough playing surfaces. With so many balls being put in play, luck was also an outsized factor. Frank Pidgeon's performance in the Fashion Course Series is a case in point. Pidgeon won game two, 29–8, thanks to excellent fielding behind him and a series of defensive mistakes by the New Yorkers. As if the baseball gods wanted to remind Pidgeon how little the pitcher mattered, in game three Brooklyn's defense had an off day (particularly catcher Folkert Boerum, who failed to stop 20 pitches), and Pidgeon lost, 29–18.

Ever since Creighton, however, pitching has been baseball's weapon of mass destruction; it is the first place to look for the reason why a baseball game was won or lost. In 1859 Creighton got banged around in his second career pitching appearance. From then on, he was all but unhittable. In 1860, Creighton won 18 games and lost two; even more impressive for an era in which batters almost always put the ball in play and fielders played barehanded, Creighton held opponents to single figures in runs sixteen times. The Eckfords did that only four times; the Atlantics did it only three times. Creighton's pitching was not only fast; it was entirely original, from his unorthodox delivery to the strange action on his pitches. Opposing hitters did not like it; they did not understand it; and some surely wondered how it could be done *without* breaking the rules.

An intriguing detail from Creighton's July 19, 1859, debut is that after Creighton began to pitch, the captain of the opposing Stars called time and huddled with the important baseball men who were in attendance. As Henry Chadwick recalled in 1869 in *The Ball Player's Chronicle*, "[The] Stars captain, after consulting several ball players present, sent in his wildest pitcher…the Stars, by these tactics, were enabled to win the game." We do not know what was said in this conversation, but we can guess. The game resumed, which means either that the Stars did not question the legality of Creighton's pitching or, if they did, they were told that Creighton's pitching was legal. More likely the Stars' captain said something similar to what Mickey Mantle said after facing Sandy Koufax in the 1963 World Series. After striking out on two high-velocity fastballs and a devastating 12–6 curve, Mantle turned to Dodgers catcher John Roseboro and complained, "How the fuck is anybody supposed to hit that shit?" To preserve their lead over the Niagaras, the frustrated Stars put in a fast wild pitcher so that neither team would be able to put the ball in play. The action ground to a halt. This is what the *New York Clipper* meant when it said that the game became "a little tedious."

Another reason to doubt that the Stars believed Creighton's pitching delivery was illegal — or might be ruled illegal — is that they immediately snatched him up and made him their everyday pitcher. After one more appearance with the Niagaras, Creighton moved up to the

Stars, along with teammate George Flanley, who was no Creighton but a future batting star. The difference that this made for the Stars is mind-boggling. Without Creighton, the Stars were the best junior club in the country—but they were still a junior club. They had defeated a respectable adult opponent earlier in the season, the Charter Oaks, but no one would have bet on them against a first-rate adult club—that is, until they got Creighton. "Having an abundance of pluck and confidence in themselves," said the *New York Times*, "they have entered the lists boldly and triumphantly against our best senior clubs." The cocky Stars challenged their elders, the Excelsiors, who agreed to play them, probably so they could test Creighton's pitching for themselves. The clubs met on Saturday, September 3rd, 1859, at the new grounds in Red Hook. Veteran Atlantic Pete O'Brien was the umpire. Creighton put up zeroes in five of the first seven innings. The grownups came back late against Creighton, but the "Little Stars" scored ten runs in the ninth to upset the Excelsiors of Leggett, Pearsall, Polhemus and Asa Brainard by a final of 17–12. Those twelve runs were the Excelsiors' lowest offensive output of the season.

Afraid of being embarrassed by Creighton and his gang of teenagers, most adult clubs were now ducking challenges from the Stars. The few senior clubs who were willing to face Creighton and the Stars were friends of the Excelsiors, the sponsors and ultimate beneficiaries of the James Creighton pitching project. The Knickerbockers stepped up, but on the condition that the Stars agree to raise the degree of difficulty by playing a "fly game." This meant that all fielders would have to catch balls in the air for an out, instead of on one bounce. The game was played in Brooklyn on September 13th. The Stars were leading, 6–3, going into the fifth inning, but a rainstorm washed out the game. The Stars played their next game on September 19th versus the Hobokens, an adult club featuring ex-Knickerbockers Otto Parisen and Norman Welling. "The match," reported the *Sunday Mercury*, "resulted pretty much as we had anticipated." James Creighton blanked the Hobokens in six of the nine innings; he allowed single runs in the second and fifth, and two in the ninth. The final score was 38–4. Allowing four runs in a nine-inning game is about average in major league baseball today, but it was an almost unthinkably low total in 1859. If we look at the 41 total games played in the 1859 season by the Eckfords, Excelsiors and Atlantics, they and their opponents scored four or fewer runs in a game only once. Both teams scored in double digits in all but five of the 41 games.

A week later the Stars took the two-ferry trip to the Elysian Fields in Hoboken, New Jersey, to make up the rained-out Knickerbocker game. The Knickerbockers scratched out a run or two here and there, but Creighton held them down until the Stars scored 18 in the eighth inning off pitcher and future brilliant Civil War general Napoleon Bonaparte McLaughlen. [What did his parents know and how did they know it?] The Stars won, 33–11. The *Sunday Mercury* wagged a finger at the boisterous crowd of Brooklyn spectators who made the trip for their "marked want of decorum" and their unseemly "hooting and shouting at the misfortunes of the Knickerbockers." The Sydney Place boys and their friends were high on the heady drug of underdog victory. "It was maintained by the Star Club," wrote Henry Chadwick, "that no one could hit Creighton's pitching."

They were wrong, but not by much. The Stars' only loss of 1859 came against the best club in baseball. The Atlantics and Stars met on October 8th and were rained out, but the non-result was an eye-opener. The Atlantics were leading, 6–5, when the rain came down, but they had the benefit of an extra turn at bat; the Stars did not get to hit in their half of the fourth. The game was made up in Brooklyn on October 19th. It was a cold, damp day, but a big crowd of six or seven thousand came out to see if the Stars really belonged on the same field as the reigning champions. According to the *Sunday Mercury,* Creighton was "'putting in' all his muscle" (throwing particularly hard) in the first inning. Lead-off hitter Pete O'Brien "couldn't get the run of his balls, and 'struck out,'" on three pitches; the next batter fouled off five or six pitches before flying out weakly to right. Then, as now, inability to make contact or to get around on pitches meant that the batter was being overpowered. The game was tied, 11–11 after seven innings, and the Atlantics won, 15–12. The difference was foolishly aggressive baserunning by the young Stars, which was deftly exploited by the Atlantics' veteran defenders. If Creighton showed any weakness, it was that once again he faded a bit late in the game. For a junior club, however, to come this close to beating the best team in baseball belongs in the moral win column. "The mettle of the Atlantics," said the *Mercury*, "was... put to the severest test."

The 1859 season ended with the Atlantics going 11–1 and threepeating as champions. Right behind them were the Eckfords, who went 11–3, two of their losses coming to the Atlantics; and the Excelsiors, who went 12–3. The upstart Stars transcended the junior classification, finishing 8–1 against adult clubs, including their upset of the Excelsiors.

The main factor in the Stars' success in 1859 was obvious: the pitching of James Creighton. What is less obvious is exactly what Creighton was doing and how he was doing it. We have no film or video of Creighton in action; and journalists' descriptions often read like a police reporter's review of an opera. Whatever it was, no umpire or baseball official ever ruled that Creighton's pitching was illegal. Apparently, there was some grumbling the following year about the legality of Creighton's pitching. We know this because Henry Chadwick responded to it. The first non-player to serve as chairman of baseball's rules committee, Chadwick's opinions carried great weight — and still do. Reporting on a game between the Putnams and Excelsiors in early August of 1860, Chadwick said: "We have heard so much of late, in baseball circles, about the pitching of Creighton, of the Excelsior Club, and its fatal effect on the scores of those who bat against it, that we determined to judge of the matter for ourselves, and accordingly we went prepared to watch his movements pretty closely, in order to ascertain whether he did pitch fairly or not, and whether his pitching was a 'jerk,' an 'underhand throw,' or a 'fair, square pitch,' and the conclusion we arrived at was, that it was unquestionably the latter." Pete O'Brien, the umpire that day, evidently agreed. "We observed," wrote Chadwick, "that P. O'Brien seemed to watch Creighton's pitching closely, and as he made no objection to its fairness." O'Brien is also a highly credible expert witness. Furthermore, as captain of the Excelsiors' arch-rivals — and as a batter who had a particularly tough time against Creighton — O'Brien would have personally benefited from Creighton's pitching being ruled illegal. We are left with the fact that *when Creighton was alive and pitching* the most sophisticated contemporary observers were 100% sure that he was not cheating.

This drawing of Creighton shows his unique one-stride, slingshot-like pitching delivery.

If James Creighton was not pitching like everyone else and he was not cheating, then what was he doing?

The first clue is that unlike every pitcher before him, Creighton did not run up to the pitching line when he delivered the ball. He took one stride, like a modern pitcher. There are hints of what his pitching motion looked like in his two surviving posed photographs, in one of which he mimics the start of his trademark delivery. His lower body is twisted like a pretzel, with his right foot turned out so that it points toward third base, and his left leg behind the right, with the foot pointing toward home plate. Creighton's toes nearly touch. In an 1860 illustration showing Creighton about to deliver a pitch, his hands are holding the ball low, at the belt, and he looks as if he is starting to twist his torso as well by closing his front shoulder and rotating his torso clockwise, away from the hitter. What we are seeing in these images is Creighton about to twist both his upper and lower body so that he can uncoil both in a coordinated way. He would load his weight onto his back leg and push off his right foot, using hip torque to generate great force, which would be conducted through the arms and hands into the baseball. As he strode forward, he achieved what modern pitching coaches call "hip-shoulder separation," which means that his lower body opened first, followed by the upper body.

This is exactly how today's pitchers achieve their velocity, except that they use a higher arm angle, and they have the added advantage of "throwing," or finishing with a whip-like motion of the arm. Creighton's motion creates arm speed, but he can only rotate a straight arm from the shoulder, not jerk his elbow straight during his delivery or, of course, snap his wrist the way all modern pitchers do. The reason why Creighton's right foot is turned out 90 degrees is to enable him to bend his right knee, get down low and release the ball from a point just above the ground. The torque of this delivery throws him off balance, which is why he finishes by putting his gloveless left hand on his front knee to steady himself.

James Creighton's pitching delivery is the product of a counterintuitive breakthrough: the realization that twisting and uncoiling the large muscles in and around the upper legs and hips generates far more power than running toward the batter. For a counterexample, we can look to cricket, where the bowler (pitcher) delivers the ball overhand as he runs toward the batsman. Pitching on the run — as opposed to pushing off a firmly planted back foot, as modern pitchers do — prevents the pitcher from closing his lower body, inhibits hip rotation and costs the pitcher speed. In first-class cricket today, a bowler who throws in the 75 mph range is called a "medium-pace bowler;" in baseball, someone who throws 75 is called a high school pitcher.

Hitters' descriptions of Creighton always lead with his bullet-like speed. His fastball is often likened to a minié ball, which was a newly invented conical bullet that was not only faster, but also more accurate and more damaging than the conventional round bullet. One Excelsior recalled seeing a Creighton pitch "striking the catcher, [causing] him to drop as if a bullet had been sent through his head.' Observers also mention his unusually low release point, which would have made his pitches hard to pick up visually and seem even faster. "[When Creighton got to work], we saw something new in [base]ball," Pete O'Brien told Henry Chadwick, "[a] low, swift delivery, the ball rising from the ground past the shoulder to the catcher."

All of James Creighton's pitches were fast and all came from the same low release point. But not all of them had the rising action that O'Brien describes. In his 1860 detailed description of Creighton's pitching, Henry Chadwick says, "We observed that whenever Creighton pitched his balls, he delivered them from within a few inches of the ground, and they rose up above the batsman's hip; and when thus delivered, the result of hitting at the ball is either to miss it or send it high in the air. The lower Creighton's balls are struck at the better they can be hit, as he cannot send in a low ball with that deceptive curve [that] he can a high one." Remember that there was universal agreement that Creighton had exceptional command of his pitches, which means that Creighton's upward movement was controlled, not the product of wildness. The only way to make sense of what Chadwick and O'Brien are describing is that Creighton intentionally threw two different pitches: one that came in around the belt and another that looked the same, but which surprised the batter by breaking high and late.

This pitch was a curveball.

Eyewitness accounts of this pitch make it sound a lot like a "riser," a breaking pitch that is thrown by softball pitchers today. You have seen baseball pitchers throw an overhand curve that "falls off the table," or breaks straight down. The riser is that same pitch turned upside down. Because it breaks sharply up, the catcher has to play closer to the batter and the plate; if he played 20 or 30 feet behind the plate, as catchers of the 1860s did when there were no men on base and fewer than two strikes on the batter, the pitch would sail over his head. Playing close to the batter is what Excelsiors catcher Joe Leggett was known for. For decades after he retired, catchers who dared to stand right behind the batter were described as "playing à la Leggett" or "Leggett-style." Joe Leggett was said to have been the first catcher to give pitching signs. This is another clue that Creighton was throwing a breaking pitch. Curveballs make it critically important for the catcher to know what pitch is coming so that he can anticipate their break. Even today, major-league catchers sometimes stop giving signs when their pitcher is throwing fastballs and changeups exclusively; they can adjust to variations in speed if they do not need to worry about too much downward or horizontal movement. The curveball is another reason why Creighton took one stride in his delivery instead of running up to the pitching line. To break off a curve, a pitcher must stop his forward movement; it is very difficult to throw a curveball while running.

If Creighton threw a curveball, why didn't Chadwick, O'Brien or anyone else say so at the time? (Why they didn't say so later is a different question with a different answer.) The answer is that they did not know what a curveball was. When something new comes into the world, its existence precedes its being given a name. We do not say, "Look, someone invented the curveball!" We say something more like, "Wait, what is that?"

Here is where it would help if there were a type of baseball around today whose pitching were similar enough to that of Creighton's time for us to use for comparison. Historians have struggled with understanding Creighton's pitching because it is so unlike the overhand pitching that has been the norm in baseball for more than a hundred years. Even though baseball pitchers in the mid-nineteenth century pitched underhand like modern softball pitchers, there are many different kinds of softball. Today's high-arc softball pitchers pitch in the 1850s sense of using a straight underhand arm motion, but because their pitches are required to reach a minimum height—usually six to twelve feet above to ground—on their way to the plate, both throwing hard and making the ball curve are impossible. Windmill and fast-pitch softball pitchers throw hard, and they use curves and other breaking pitches, but they "throw" in the 1850s sense; they use a whipping arm motion, pronating the forearm, breaking the wrist and "jerking" the arm straight. This was, of course, illegal when Creighton played. Remember that according to Henry Chadwick and Pete O'Brien—and all other available contemporary eyewitnesses—Creighton did not do that. When I was doing research for this book, however, I discovered that there is a living variety of softball whose pitching rules are uncannily similar to those that Creighton pitched under.

Meet my friend Sal Guerriero. A former New York City high school baseball coach, Sal has been a softball pitcher for more than fifty years, but his passion for the game is ageless. He belongs to a legendary family athletic dynasty on Staten Island, where he grew up. Sal's father played professional baseball; his oldest brother was an outstanding amateur football and softball player, and his four nieces were all 1000-point scorers in New York City high school basketball, as well as being outstanding softball players. His other brother was a D1 athlete in both baseball and basketball and threw a no-hitter in the American Legion World Series. I reached Sal through his website, 10manmodified.com. The purpose of the site is to promote and defend a variety of softball called "10-man modified." Once known as "medium pitch," 10-man modified is recognized by the Amateur Softball Association and is currently played in New York, New Jersey, eastern Pennsylvania and in other parts of the United States. The pitching is underhand and fast-ish, but pitching velocity is limited in two ways: by restricting the height of the backswing and by making it illegal for pitchers to hold the ball outside of the wrist. Under 10-man modified rules, the pitcher's backswing cannot go higher than a roughly 90-degree angle to an imaginary line drawn from the hip to the shoulder to the hand; and he cannot pronate the forearm, because that would cock the wrist and position the ball on the outside, that is, the side away from the pitcher's body; this makes windmilling or any kind of throwing or disguised throwing impossible, including the arm motion that Creighton's contemporaries in the 1860s called throwing. If this is too confusing, try picking up a baseball and pitching it dead underhand without pronating the forearm or cocking the wrist; you will see that the backswing naturally stops at about 90 degrees; you will also see that you cannot snap your wrist or straighten a bent elbow (i.e., "jerk") during the delivery. If you practice for a while, you might be able to break 45 mph on a radar gun. Ten-man modified pitchers take a single stride and deliver the ball underhand, with the arm straight and without cocking the wrist. Hmmm.

Sal Guerriero throwing the "no-throw" underhand rising curveball using the fingers to generate spin à la James Creighton

When Sal showed me his pitching motion, I noticed that he would twist his upper body clockwise, drop down and release the ball from just above his shoe tops, just as Creighton did. Like Henry Chadwick, I saw no violation of the pitching rules that Creighton played under. Sal asked me to give it a try. I swung my arm back, turned my forearm and held the ball with my palm facing second base. "No!" Sal yelled. "You can't do that!" My instinctive underhand throwing motion resembled not that of the unhittable Creighton, but rather the motion used by the baseball pitchers of the 1870s—the decade when the baseball rule makers and umpires gave up trying to enforce the rule against throwing and, not coincidentally, when every pitcher learned the curveball. Almost anyone can learn how to throw a curveball if they can snap their wrist; doing it without snapping the wrist is much, much harder. I asked Sal how he made the ball curve without "throwing," and he showed me. He holds the ball with his wrist straight and aligned with the forearm (the throwing hand in a handshake position but pointing down), and with his hand on the outside of the ball, away from the body. When he releases the pitch, he grips the ball tightly with his fingertips and spins the ball by quickly flipping the fingers upward; if done with enough strength and coordination, the ball will rotate enough that the ball will break sharply upward, 6–12 fashion.

The cause of the break is the Magnus effect—the same aerodynamic phenomenon that makes an overhand baseball curve break down, sideways or both. It is named after Heinrich Gustave Magnus, a German scientist who in 1853 wanted to find out why cannonballs curved in the air. The *Encyclopedia Brittanica* defines the Magnus effect as the "generation of a sidewise force on a spinning cylindrical or spherical solid immersed in a fluid (liquid or gas) when there is relative motion between the spinning body and the fluid." Thinking that it would be easier to see it than to figure out what that means, I met Sal in McGolrick Park, near my house in Greenpoint, Brooklyn, let him warm up and watched him throw his straight-arm, no wrist snap riser to my son Wes, who played college baseball and who has seen plenty of curveballs. It was easy to see how helpless Pete O'Brien must have felt when he faced Creighton. Clearly expecting the ball to come in slower and knee-high, Wes leaped up from his catcher's crouch, speared the ball with both feet off the ground, landed, shook his head and laughed.

Sal did not enter our conversation knowing a thing about James Creighton or nineteenth-century baseball pitching, but the more we talked, the more I felt like I was time tripping back to 1860. Like Creighton, he needed to push off a firmly planted back foot. When

Sal was playing on poorly maintained public fields, he told me that he made sure to show up early with a pitching rubber, board and tools. "I used to dig a hole and put in a concrete block, rubber or a piece of wood, so I had something to drive off of. The pitch flattens out if you can't push." Contemporary accounts confirm that Creighton needed to push off his back foot to be effective. Reporting on a June 1862 game, the *New York Clipper* explained a below-par performance by Creighton by saying, "Creighton was not suited with the ground, a firm footing being one of the prerequisites to give due effect to his pitching…." Asked to elaborate on the rising curve, Sal said, "The key to a riser is spin rate—you need to get the 6–12 rotation and enough speed. In baseball, of course, the classic curve is 12–6. My riser was all fingers, not even a wrist turn. You are controlling it with just fingers, which takes a lot of strength and a lot of technique." (A *Sunday Mercury* article from 1860 notes Creighton's odd way of holding the baseball *with his fingertips*). "If Creighton is doing the same thing, it wouldn't look illegal under those [1860] rules, right? The ball is never outside the wrist, and it is never jerked."

Sal added, "Back in the day there was only one person in the country that threw this pitch this way—me. And even I had a hard time throwing it consistently. I could try to teach it to you. You would have to throw it thousands of times against a wall and work through a lot of failure before you get it. Even if you get the break, it is very hard to control. Think about how few true, high-quality 12–6 curves you see in baseball today—the old Lord Charles—you know what I'm saying?" I know exactly what Sal was saying. Even for accomplished major-league pitchers, it is one thing to spin a curve so that it breaks 12–6; it is another thing—a much harder thing—to control and locate this kind of pitch. Without command it is virtually useless, because even if it has consistent sharp break, batters will simply take it for a ball. This is what Henry Chadwick was talking about in 1860 when he said about Creighton, "The idea of mere speed alone making a swiftly pitched ball a difficult one to hit…is nonsense to us…. Speed is not the difficulty; it is something else, and that something else is…*judging the difference between balls coming straight to the bat and those coming with curved lines.*" Chadwick lived until 1908 and whenever someone said that the latest hard-throwing phenom "warn't no Creighton," he would tell them that it was not speed alone that made Creighton unhittable, but the combination of speed, movement and control. More than a century later, this is still the definition of effective pitching.

Let's talk speed. How fast was James Creighton throwing? We do not have radar gun readings, obviously, but we have a couple of reference points that we can use to make an educated guess. Tom Browning figured that he could throw 40–50 mph using the pre-Creighton running up and pitching delivery. Using the more efficient single stride delivery à la Creighton, Sal Guerriero estimates that he threw 65 mph. I will buy that, too. James Creighton was far shorter than Sal, but Creighton was a superstar athlete who dominated baseball at the highest level. When he took up cricket, he went from a novice to a first-rate bowler in a matter of months. It is not crazy to wonder if Creighton was the best athlete in the United States in 1860. Perhaps we should ask the question this way: how hard would a world-class, all-around athlete like a Michael Jordan, a Bo Jackson or a Jim Thorpe throw if he mastered 10-man modified pitching—70 mph? 75 mph? There is one other factor to account for: pitching distance. Like Guerriero, Creighton delivered the ball from about 43 feet from the batter's contact point. It is simple math to calculate the mph equivalent for a pitch thrown from today's baseball pitching distance, which averages about 54 feet from the pitcher's hand to the bat. A 10-man modified batter facing Sal Guerriero or a hitter from 1860 facing Creighton throwing 65 mph has the same time to react to the pitch as a modern batter facing a fastball traveling at 94 mph. If James Creighton was throwing 70 mph, the number rises to 101.1 mph—Aroldis Chapman territory. Creighton could have been throwing that hard. He also could have been throwing harder.

Did James Creighton invent the curveball? There are many pretenders to the title of first curveball pitcher; all of them have their believers. Was it slow-throwing control pitcher Alphonse Martin of the old Mutuals and Eckfords? Fred Goldsmith? Bobby Mathews? There are too many credible candidates to list. None of the usual suspects, however, claimed to have thrown the curve before 1860. Still, the question is far from settled. To prove that someone did something first, of course, involves accomplishing the almost impossible feat of proving a negative — that no one had ever done that thing at any earlier time. History, however, is made out of stories, not logic. If you have been to the National Baseball Hall of Fame in Cooperstown, New York, you know that the generally accepted originator — the Abner Doubleday of the curveball — is William Arthur Cummings (known today as "Candy," he was "Arthur" when he said he invented the curve in the middle or late 1860s). The more you learn about baseball in the 1860s, the more you suspect that Cummings is credited with inventing the curveball mainly because he told a good story. They say in marketing that to sell a product, you need a story; and a good story is better than a true story. Cummings's went like this: one day when he was a boy, he was throwing clamshells on a Brooklyn beach (no, not Coney Island; he probably meant the banks of the Gowanus, near where Cummings lived); he was fascinated by how they swerved and swooped in the air, and it occurred to him that it might be possible to make a baseball behave in a similar way. This makes no sense if you think about it for a few minutes, but if you don't, it has a superficial plausibility.

What pitcher invented the curveball, however, may be the wrong question. Somebody threw the first curve, but that somebody would have been working in close partnership with a catcher, so the answer would almost certainly be two names, not one. This makes it interesting to say the least that Candy Cummings's curveball invention tale entirely leaves out his first catcher, Joe Leggett, the man who discovered, recruited, trained and mentored him. Debates over the inventor of the curveball consistently overlook the key fact that pitching is by its nature collaborative. The pitcher is important, but so is his partner squatting sixty feet away. There is a reason why for 150 years pitcher and catcher have been called a "battery." Any baseball fan knows that catchers encourage, teach — sometimes even think for — their pitchers.

Thanks to advancing technology, we can now measure how much fine points of catching such as pitch calling and framing affect pitching outcomes. It has also been true going all the way back to the nineteenth century that a pitcher is limited not only by his stuff, but also by the catcher's ability to handle his stuff. This part of catching was an even greater factor in James Creighton's time, when catchers had no gloves or protective equipment. To put it simply, if Joe Leggett couldn't stop it, then Creighton—and Cummings—couldn't throw it.

Joseph Leggett was serving as a volunteer firefighter with Pacific Engine Company #14 in Brooklyn Heights when his baseball club, the Waynes, merged with the Excelsiors in 1857. Dr. Joseph Jones became president of the Excelsiors that same year. Considering that Jones operated the only gymnasium in Brooklyn in the 1850s (about five blocks from Pacific #14), it is hard to imagine that they did not already know each other through their common interest in gymnastics, boxing and weightlifting. The two men ran the Excelsiors and jointly created a plan to build a championship club and to use that club to spread and promote baseball. Both of them were older than the rest of the players of the Excelsiors' starters, or "first nine." Born in 1828, Leggett turned 32 before the 1860 season, when Flanley and Creighton were 19-year-olds. There were no field managers in baseball at that time, but Leggett was the nearest thing; as team captain he directed the other players on the field. Off the field, he arranged their games and tours and policed the clubhouse. On the club's 1860 trip to Baltimore, Leggett made his players promise not to stay out late or touch alcohol. (All of them except first baseman Aleck Pearsall kept their promise.) Leggett was also the author of the Excelsiors' rigorous training regimen. The Excelsiors practiced three times a week instead of the normal two, and trained with weights, which was also unusual, possibly unique, in that time. In modern baseball terminology, Joe Leggett held the jobs of starting catcher, manager, field captain, trainer, pitching coach—and scout. Leggett caught James Creighton, Asa Brainard and Candy Cummings, but he was also the man who saw their potential as pitchers, trained and developed them. When Leggett first met them, Creighton and Brainard were infielders; when he first met Cummings, Cummings was a teenager. Leggett spotted Cummings pitching for a junior club, invited him to practice with the Excelsiors, and convinced Cummings's parents to allow their son to play with an adult club. Leggett later named a son after Cummings.

Not all of the details of the relationships between Leggett and his pitchers are accessible to us. Most of what happened between them took place during practices, outside the view of the newspaper reporters that we rely on for most of what we know about Amateur Era baseball. But we can get a general idea by piecing together contemporary newspaper stories, later reminiscences and a bit of context. We do not know if Joe Leggett personally found or recruited James Creighton, but it is possible, especially considering that Leggett later recruited Cummings as a minor. When the Excelsiors brought Creighton to Brooklyn and managed his progress through their affiliated junior clubs, the club was co-run by Leggett. In 1916, newspapers published the memoirs of an old ballplayer named Jimmy Wood. Wood played for the Eckfords of Greenpoint from 1859 to the mid-1860s; he later had a professional career in Chicago and died in California, but he was about the same age as James Creighton and played in Brooklyn at the same time. He recalled that Leggett came up with a novel pitching drill for Creighton. Wood says that this took place after Creighton joined the Excelsiors, but it probably happened earlier; Creighton was close to a finished product when he was with the Stars. "Jimmy," Wood remembered Leggett saying, "speed is the thing. You've got a lot of it, but I want you to have more when the next season opens. Therefore, I want you to get an iron ball, the same size as a baseball, and pitch it for at least a half hour each day during the winter [presumably against a barrier — not even Joe Leggett could catch an iron baseball]. That will develop your muscles and your speed as well." Remember that Sal Guerriero told me that the way to master the no-throw underhand rising curve was reps — throwing it over, and over again, against a wall.

We rightly take stories told by old ballplayers long after the fact with a grain of salt. But there are patterns to the distortions of human memory. People tend to exaggerate, minimize or even invent events and details, but they do so to conform their memories to the conventional wisdom, because they have an axe to grind, or for another reason. What they do not generally do, is invent an apparently trivial or meaningless detail for no reason. Jimmy Wood's story about Leggett telling Creighton to throw weighted baseballs is believable because it does not reinforce an existing narrative, serves no personal agenda of Wood's, and above all, because Wood himself was not aware of its significance. In his words, it was "the strangest plan ever known." To throw a curveball under the rules that James Creighton played under required both great strength, coordination and flexibility, and the know-how to create a new pitching delivery and a new training regimen — in short, both

An illustration from Harry Ellard's 1907 Baseball in Cincinnati *showing that Asa Brainard's pitching delivery was an exact replica of James Creighton's.*

a gifted athlete and a visionary coach. The teenage James Creighton filled the first part of this bill, but he had no theoretical knowledge of pitching technique or physical training. Joe Leggett did.

After James Creighton died in 1862, the Excelsiors replaced him with backup infielder Asa Brainard. Brainard's pitching delivery was identical to Creighton's. Brainard took one stride, had a low release point, and finished with his left hand on his front knee. Like Creighton, he threw very hard. Did he have Creighton's curveball? Not according to standard baseball histories or the Hall of Fame, but Harry Wright, recalling the days when he managed Brainard with the Cincinnati Red Stockings, said, "Asa's toss had all sorts of twists with it; twists that evaded the onslaught of the batsman and rendered him incapable of inflicting an assault on the sphere beyond pop flies." It is hard to be sure whether what Wright calls "twist" is a breaking pitch or something else. But in 1886, ballplayer Jack Nelson (who was also nicknamed "Candy" late in his career) gave an interview to the Louisville, Kentucky *Courier*. Playing for the Eckfords and the New York Mutuals from 1867 through 1870, Nelson faced Brainard, who pitched in 1867 for the Washington Nationals and afterward for the famed Cincinnati Red Stockings. Nelson is sharp and unsentimental; there is no trace of the fogginess on detail or old-fogeyism that you see when veteran players talk about old times. When asked if the players of his youth were better than those of the 1880s, Nelson replied: "This is ridiculous. Why, if the old Eckfords were resurrected and play as good as they ever did, they wouldn't stand a ghost of a show against the clubs of the League or American Association." He went on to the subject of Asa Brainard, unprompted: "[Brainard] was about the only pitcher that had any curves in his delivery, but he didn't know it. For a long time, the boys couldn't hit him, and none of them could tell what was the reason. It was finally discovered, though, that he had a little curve, and his pitching therefore couldn't be gauged. Arthur Cummings was another of the old-timers, and *among the first pitchers* that curved the ball." [italics mine]

It sounds strange that Brainard would not know that he was throwing a curve, but it raises questions of taxonomy that lurk in any discussion, contemporary or historical, of who threw the first curve. A lot depends on what we mean by curve. Some dictionaries, for example, define a curveball not only as a pitch that spins and breaks, but as a breaking pitch that breaks down, or horizontally and down. By this definition, James Creighton could not have thrown a curveball because his pitch broke upward. A less arbitrary definition of the curveball is a pitch whose spin makes it curve in the air (in any direction) because of the Magnus effect. This definition is broad enough to include sliders and other breaking pitches, but these pitches are kin to the curveball. They may look different to the hitter, but they all break because of the same aerodynamic phenomenon. There is no bright line between them; sometimes even baseball experts are not sure whether to call a particular breaking pitch a curve or a slider—or a slurve. Before the 1950s or 60s, when pitchers learned how devastating it could be when paired correctly with the fastball, the slider was derided as a "nickel curve." It is perfectly plausible that Joe Leggett and James Creighton came up with something like Sal Guerriero's rising curveball and that Leggett taught Asa Brainard how to make a pitch break in a similar way without any of the three understanding the science of why it curved or even what to call it. All they had to know was how to throw it and that it got hitters out.

In 1865, when Joe Leggett saw Arthur Cummings pitching for a youth club affiliated with the Stars, Leggett was at the end of the line as a ballplayer. Years of lunging for pitches in the dirt, throwing out baserunners, and catching Creighton barehanded left him with mangled fingers, a bad leg and a bad shoulder. But he could still recognize athletic potential, and he could still teach. Leggett and Cummings played together with the Excelsiors in 1866, Cummings occasionally substituting for Asa Brainard. By 1867, Brainard had gone to Washington and Leggett was washed up. Cummings became the regular pitcher for the Leggett-less Excelsiors and then pitched for the Stars (who had become a senior club in 1860). Cummings was one of the finest pitchers in late Amateur Era baseball until throwing too many curveballs wrecked his arm. He had a solid, if less spectacular, career in the professional National Association and pitched one season in the National League with the Cincinnati Reds. Can it be a coincidence that Creighton, Brainard and Cummings were all, for a time, the best pitchers in the game; that all three of them threw curveballs before they became common; and that all three were caught, coached and trained by the same man?

Arthur "Candy" Cummings demonstrating his pitching delivery years after the fact. He is clearly pronating his forearm in order to deliver the baseball with an illegal "throw."

Creighton and Brainard may have been better at pitching, but Cummings was better at marketing. In 1887, *Boston Globe* sportswriter and ex-pitcher Tim Murnane printed a story that Cummings told him of how he discovered the curveball. "Cummings," he writes, "was the first to bring into use the out curve ... He was pitching against a picked nine one day [in 1869] and noticed the ball curving... He went home that night and tried to study out the phenomenon... He learned that the curve came from a certain twist he gave the wrist." Cummings embellished the story over the years—note the late date and the absence of flying clam shells—but this version is at least plausible. Baseball history is full of stories about pitchers hitting upon a new technique or a new pitch by inadvertently changing their grip or arm angle. Cummings is probably telling the truth about snapping his wrist, because "throwing" was illegal in 1869, as it was in Creighton's day. People do not normally lie when they are admitting to cheating. While the rule against "throwing" was not being consistently enforced in 1869, Cummings also confessed that he disguised his wrist snap to hide it from umpires. In the Brooklyn *Daily Eagle* of April 26, 1896, Cummings told a different story of how, after practicing for some time, he threw his first effective curveball while playing for the Excelsiors against a Harvard College team in 1867. If this really happened, no newspaper reporter who was there noticed it. Cummings lost that game, 18–6.

By 1908, Cummings had perfected his creation tale by throwing in the clam shells and moving his early experiments in throwing the curve to 1864, when he was attending prep school in upstate New York. While the young Cummings attracted attention for his pitching velocity, there is no contemporary mention of him making the ball do anything other than move very fast until 1870, when several game stories remark on the unusual sideways break of Cummings's curveball. It is described as an "out curve," a "side-curve" or a "sailing-type pitch," meaning that it broke on a horizontal plane, not upwards. Cummings's innovation was that he could make it break both away from and into a right-handed batter. This was something that James Creighton could not have done under the rules as they were enforced in his day. "Just as the curved line of a tossed ball bothers the sight of a batsman," writes the *New York Clipper* of January 1, 1875, "so does the side curve of a swiftly pitched ball, such as Matthews and Cummings send in when they put on their speed. The reason that this style is so difficult to punish is that the batsman is led to expect that the ball is coming close to him, while, instead, it curves out from him, and vice-versa." These stories confirm that Cummings was using a wrist throw in violation of the rules. The only way for a righthanded pitcher to make the curve break away from a righthanded batter is to snap the wrist. The other thing they tell us is that Cummings was using a higher arm angle than Creighton. This also makes sense; pitchers of the late 1860s and 1870s were pushing hard against the rule that outlawed raising the arm angle above dead underhand. The curve was the reason—the higher the arm angle, the more effective the curve.

In 1918, newspaper sports sections once again took up the "curve ball controversy." The *New York Sun* ran a story in which an unnamed source claimed that he had been told personally by Arthur Cummings that Cummings "got the idea" of the curveball from none other than James Creighton. In response, the sports editor of the *Evening Wisconsin* newspaper tracked down Herbert Jewell, who had caught Cummings after Leggett and who then lived in Milwaukee. Jewell dismissed the story, but his arguments are weak. Jewell said that Cummings was a "very small boy" when Creighton died and that it would have been impossible for Cummings to have talked with Creighton or even to have seen him pitch. In fact, Cummings turned 14 on the day of Creighton's death. Jewell must have known that; he was 17 in 1862 and the two were neighbors. At the time, both Jewell and Cummings lived blocks from Creighton's house and played baseball together in nearby Carroll Park. Jewell added that "George Flanley, a friend of Creighton's and myself were quite intimate for many years, and he never mentioned the fact...that Creighton had produced a curved ball." This may be true but not mentioning that Creighton threw a curve is hardly the same as saying that he did not. Jewell's account is also open to a perfectly reasonable alternative interpretation, that Flanley—like almost everyone else who saw Creighton pitch—did not understand what he was looking at.

It is also consistent with another plausible scenario, that Cummings did adapt Creighton's curveball, but that the result looked so different—it was "thrown" with a wrist snap; it was thrown from a different arm angle; and it broke horizontally, not up—that it was perceived to be a new pitch. In 1937, a suburban New Jersey real estate broker named Parkes saw an article in the Brooklyn *Daily Eagle* about the recently established baseball Hall of Fame. He was annoyed to read that Arthur Cummings was going to be admitted to the Hall for having invented the curveball. He sent in a letter to the editor saying, "an uncle of mine...discovered the first curved ball, although at that time they didn't know just what it was." The writer's full name was James Creighton Parkes. His uncle was James Creighton.

Arthur Cummings had an excellent baseball career, but that is not why he is in the Hall of Fame. He is there because a three-man committee of two league presidents and Commissioner Kenesaw Mountain

Landis decided that he threw the first curveball. It is no great surprise that they got it wrong. James Creighton's pitching baffled contemporary observers, who did not know that he was throwing a curveball, and they can be forgiven for not realizing that Arthur Cummings's strange-looking pitch was simply a different kind of curveball. It helped that Cummings lived until 1924 and was a popular figure in professional baseball in the late nineteenth century, when sportswriters began to look back and ask who threw the first curve. The irony is that James Creighton, who pitched within the rules, has been denied the credit he deserves for throwing the first curve; while Cummings, who cheated to throw his curveball, has a bronze plaque in Cooperstown.

Game one of the 1860 series between the Atlantics and Excelsiors in Red Hook, Brooklyn. Estimated at 12,000, at the time this was the largest baseball crowd ever. With James Creighton in top form, the Excelsiors won, 23–4.

1860

IT LOOKED LIKE 1860 was the year that someone was finally going to take down the Atlantics. The Atlantics were not going to be easy to beat. Since the founding of the National Association, they had lost three games. They had never lost a three-game series. The 1860 Eckfords were good enough to do it, but the Excelsiors were coming with the deadliest weapon in baseball—peak James Creighton.

Before the season began, however, the news broke that the Excelsiors were planning something else that no club had done before: a multi-city baseball road trip. "A Grand Excursion in Contemplation," announced the Brooklyn *Daily Eagle* in late April, "The plan is to arrange a series of matches with clubs in the interior [i.e., upstate New York], and play them in succession...If circumstances permit, the excursion may be extended to Baltimore and Washington, stopping at Philadelphia on the way home...it would add greatly to the advancement of the popularity of the game of baseball."

Today, road trips are part of the normal rhythm of a baseball season. When you think about it, a professional schedule is essentially a series of road trips. The Excelsiors' 1860 trips were the first. They bore little resemblance to the modern version. In the pre–Civil War era, when one amateur club visited another, the action continued after the final out of the game. The home club was obliged to wine and dine the visitors. For the more socially elevated clubs, this meant pulling out all the stops: a formal postgame banquet with speeches, toasts, brandy and cigars. Sometimes the party lasted until dawn. And the Excelsiors were not going upstate in pursuit of a championship. There was no such thing as a baseball league or a schedule in 1860, and championships were not determined by won-lost record. Clubs became champions by challenging and defeating the incumbent champion in a three-game series. The reason for their travels lay in the Excelsiors' deeper purpose as an organization — to make the New York game the game for all Americans. Dr. Jones and his baseball missionaries helped found new clubs in Buffalo, Baltimore, Washington DC, Montgomery, Alabama and Richmond, Virginia. They did so for the same reason that they made the baseball tours of 1860 and 1862 — not for themselves but for the cause of baseball.

The Excelsiors were not introducing the game to upstate New York. Baseball had a foundation there and in other areas that had cultural and economic connections to New York City. Loyalist refugees had brought a primitive version of baseball to southern Ontario after the American Revolution. The Gold Rush brought baseball 1840s-style to northern California. The game also spread along with commerce to the Upper Midwest via the Erie Canal, to New Orleans with the cotton trade and elsewhere. Baseball went to school with New York students who attended prep schools and colleges in New England. (The first Harvard baseball club was formed by undergraduates from New York and Brooklyn). This is why the Excelsiors had no trouble finding baseball clubs to play in Albany, Rochester and Buffalo. In the summer of 1860, most of them were newly organized, but the upstate clubs were paying attention to what was happening in New York City and Brooklyn. They were eager to join the party and get up to speed.

James Creighton's first appearance of 1860 was in an impromptu contest of mixed sides including Excelsiors, Charter Oaks and two gentlemen who were in town for the annual national baseball convention, held in mid-March at Cooper Union in Manhattan. They were delegates from the Excelsior Club of Baltimore, which was named after the Brooklyn club because Joe Leggett and Harry Polhemus had helped found it. James Creighton played first base, which tells us how little it mattered who won this game. It was followed on April 19th by another preseason tune-up. Billed as "Leggett's Side" versus "Whiting's Side," this was a novelty contest between the Excelsiors' frontline players and their organization men. Appearing for the Whitings were future Civil War hero, Colorado rancher and politician Benjamin Kimberley; Charles Gulick; Richard Oliver; and Charles Whiting—all energetic baseball proselytizers. The Leggetts had first-nine starters Polhemus, Flanley, Pearsall, Russell, Leggett and Creighton, who pitched. To no one's surprise, the Leggetts won, 21–3.

The something crazy happened. The Excelsiors dropped their first real game of the 1860 season, 12–11, to the Charter Oaks, a club full of old friends of the Excelsiors that was one or two competitive notches beneath them. This was not a one-off; a year earlier, the Charter Oaks had also upset the Excelsiors in the first game of the season, also by one run. Was this a case of corrupt manipulation of the betting odds, spring training-itis or simply what Henry Chadwick liked to call "the glorious uncertainty" of baseball? In the 1860 game James Creighton gave up a lot of runs—for him—including four in the late innings. To be fair to Creighton, it was his season pitching debut, his defense was shaky, and the game was no work of art. The Charter Oaks' home field in Carroll Park was cramped and short on outfield and foul territory, so outfielders running down long fly balls had to deal with sidewalks, spectators and lamp posts. The two runs that won the game for the Oaks scored on a routine fly ball to left that, according to the *New York Clipper*, Excelsior left fielder Ed Russell "lost in the crowd." This game turned out to be a minor blot on a near-perfect season; it was the Excelsiors' only loss of 1860 that did not come at the hands of the Atlantics. In a rematch with the Charter Oaks one month later, the Excelsiors cleaned up Dodge—and lightened the wallets of those who bet against them. They led 16–0 after two innings and coasted to a 36–9 laugher.

On Saturday evening, June 30th, the Excelsiors boarded the 405-foot-long *Isaac Newton* or another of the steamships that plied the fjord that we call the lower Hudson River. Called "floating palaces," sleek paddle wheelers like the *Newton* reached 25 mph—world-record speed for the time—and made the 150-mile overnight trip to Albany, including stops, in time for breakfast the next day. The Excelsiors were not saving time or money; the train was cheaper and faster. They travelled by boat to bathe in the transcendent beauty of the Hudson. In 1860, a visiting member of Parliament described the trip as "one of the finest of its kind in the world; and it is greatly enhanced by the size and beauty of the boats on which you make the trip, and the conveniences, and luxury, of their apartments. The view of the city...is in itself, with its domes and spires and busy hum of life, a sight of considerable interest.... Sailing rapidly past...we soon reach the 'Palisades,' precipices which rise in some places 500 feet above the river...richly wooded on their summits." On their way to Albany, passengers would pass through the magical Tappan Zee (then unmarred by the New York State Thruway), glide by majestic West Point and Storm King mountains; and watch the Catskills turn blue in the haze of a summer evening.

The fast steamer Armenia, *built in 1847 for the Hudson River route between New York City and Albany.*

There was no baseball on Sundays in 1860. The Excelsiors took the field on Monday against the Champion Club of Albany. Fielding their best nine, minus slugger George Flanley, a telegraphic engineer with the Brooklyn Police Department who could not get the time off, the Excelsiors won easily, 24–6. The *Sunday Mercury* wrote that "Creighton's pitches were...as swift as they could be sent from a cannon, and they were most difficult to [hit]... Joe Leggett...caught superbly—not a ball passing him." After the game, both clubs headed to the Merchants' Hotel for the post-game spread. The Excelsiors spent that night at Albany's ritziest hotel, the Stanwix, which had been built in 1833 by a grandfather and great-uncle of Herman Melville, author of *Moby Dick*. The Stanwix had an elegant marble façade, a majestic rooftop ballroom and sky-high room rates.

Lopsided victories, fine dining and breathless accounts of the Brooklyn club's awe-inspiring athleticism were the themes of the coverage of the rest of the Excelsiors' upstate tour, with one exception. On July 3rd, the Victory Club of Troy, across the Hudson from Albany, held the Excelsiors to a surprisingly low 13 runs; Troy scored seven off Creighton to make it a very respectable loss. This looked more like a fluke then than it does in retrospect. A muscular industrial hub, nineteenth-century Troy produced iron, textiles, shirt collars—and athletes. In 1860 the two-year-old future MLB superstar Mike "King" Kelly (presumably still drinking milk) was living near Weir's Course, where the Victories played. Troy would also give birth to the great Troy Haymakers club, which was cofounded by some of the same men who played for the Victory club against the Excelsiors. Sponsored by boxing politician and bookmaker John Morrissey, a son of Troy, the Haymakers became one of the top clubs in the country in the late 1860s. After their victory over the Victory Club, the Excelsiors freshened up and reassembled at the Troy House hotel for the nightcap. We have a menu from a similar Troy House banquet from 1863. Diners warmed up with mock turtle soup, baked fish and cold roast meats; next up were veal pot pie, escalloped oysters and boiled lobster. These were followed in the order by hot roast beef, mutton, pork, turkey, duck and goose; side orders of rice, mashed potatoes and greens crossed the plate as well. The closer was a dessert buffet of nuts, fruit and lemon ice cream. The next day, the Brooklyn baseball tourists celebrated America's 84th birthday by dragging themselves to the New York Central railroad station and catching the train to Buffalo, a hot and dusty eight hours to the west.

They were welcomed in Buffalo by the Niagara Club. The Excelsiors had helped organize the Niagaras through two members with family connections to Buffalo: James Bach and Richard Oliver, who along with Joe Leggett had come to the Excelsiors in the 1857 Wayne Club merger. Benjamin Kimberley was also involved; he lived in Brooklyn but was born in Batavia, New York, forty-five miles from Buffalo. He guest-umpired an 1859 game between the Niagaras and the Erie club. As one paper put it, the "Niagaras look upon the Excelsiors as their parent club." The Niagaras took the visitors to dinner on the Fourth and escorted them to Niagara Falls for an overnight stay at the prestigious Clifton House on the Canadian side.

On July 5th, the Excelsiors gave their offspring a good spanking, 50–19. The Excelsiors scored 10 runs in the fourth inning and—no typo—24 runs in the fifth. The locals were shell-shocked. A Buffalo paper wrote:

> It is safe to say that no such ball playing was ever before witnessed in Buffalo. The manner in which the Excelsiors handled the ball, the ease with which they caught it...the precision with which they threw it to the bases, and the tremendous hits they gave it to the long field made the optics of the Buffalo players glisten with admiration and protrude with amazement...Some were, without doubt, a little discouraged.

The following day the Excelsiors took the train to Rochester, where they passed the time between bouts of gluttony by pasting the Flour City Club 21–1, and taking down the Live Oaks, 27–9.

Local newspapers were generally philosophical about all this losing. The Buffalo *Commercial Advertiser* was more grudging. "The Excelsior first nine," it complained, "is made up of men culled from other clubs, until there is not a second-rate player among them." The first part of that sentence is unfair. "The Niagaras," continued the paper, "were well aware of the character of their antagonists, expected to be beaten, and bore their flogging with good grace." Hoping to give the Excelsiors a better game, the Niagaras had built temporary wooden stands that were packed by four thousand people, by far the largest baseball crowd in Buffalo history. A Rochester paper described the Excelsiors' bleaching of the Flour City club as follows: "The fact became apparent very soon after the playing began, that the Flour City had no chance whatever—the Excelsiors having things pretty much their own way...The fact that the Rochester boys made only one run was owing less to their own want of skill than to the remarkable amount of it possessed by the Excelsiors."

The Excelsiors' final stop was Newburgh, New York, sixty-five miles upriver from New York City. Fellow club members and friends met the Excelsiors at the Orange Hotel and celebrated the club's homecoming from their triumphal upstate march. The Excelsiors were banged up and visibly exhausted after travelling 1000 miles by train, boat and coach, playing five games in six days, and eating and drinking like kings. Joe Leggett caught Creighton although "damaged in the way of fingers." They defeated the Hudson River club of Newburgh anyway, 59–14. It could have been even worse; Ed Russell came in for Creighton in the ninth and allowed five of Newburgh's 14 runs. Totaling up the numbers from all six games of the tour, the Excelsiors scored 194 runs to their opponents' 56, "most of the runs made off [Creighton]," according to Henry Chadwick, "the result of loose fielding on the part of the Excelsiors." Joe Leggett scored the most runs of any individual player, 26, followed by Creighton and John Whiting at 25. Catcher Leggett was outstanding on defense, allowing five passed balls to the Niagaras' 11, one passed ball to the Flour City's nine, and one passed ball to the Hudson River club catcher's 22. James Creighton was the winning pitcher in every game.

The upstate New York leg of the Excelsiors' baseball mission infected the entire region with baseball fever. New clubs sprang up like asparagus in May. Within a few years, many of them were competitive on a national level. Seventy-three New York State clubs attended the national baseball convention in New York City in 1866, the most of any state. Other parts of America, however, played their own bat-and-ball games, which made them a harder nut to crack. America also had many cricket-playing first-generation English immigrants; there were hundreds of American cricket clubs in 1860. Philadelphia had town ball, its own homegrown bat-and-ball game; the oldest town ball club, the Olympics, went back to 1831. The Massachusetts game, native to Boston and Massachusetts east of the Berkshires, also had deep roots. The English were a hopeless case, but the Excelsiors were sure that when Americans in those places experienced for themselves the exciting and athletic game played by Creighton and his teammates, they would convert to the one true faith of baseball. They were not wrong.

On Friday evening, September 21st, 1860, James Creighton and the Excelsiors crossed the Hudson River to Jersey City, New Jersey, where they caught the night train to Baltimore. They pulled in at four in the morning and were met by members of the Baltimore Excelsior Club and taken to Guy's Monument House for "a splendid breakfast." Located on Monument Square, named for a memorial to men who died in the war of 1812, Guy's was a 150-room hotel with a kitchen that stood out even in a fine dining mecca like Baltimore. One nineteenth-century guide called Guy's turtle soup "as fine... as any epicure could desire;" another wrote that "terrapin and soft-shelled crab are served there in all the glory and perfection of Baltimore cookery." That afternoon, the Excelsiors were picked up by a special horse-drawn coach that was gaily festooned with flags, and driven to the baseball grounds, where an immense crowd had turned out for the game. The *New York Clipper* reported that the spectators included "a large delegation of the fashionable belles of the city," who were so fascinating to Asa Brainard, John Whiting and Tom Reynolds in particular that Captain Leggett could be heard sharply reminding them to focus on baseball.

When the game began, it was the home team's turn to be distracted. "The preliminary practice," wrote the *Clipper*, "had given their opponents a foretaste of what there was in reserve for them... one, two, three was the order of their going out, while the Brooklynites gave them some ideas in the way of run getting." *Wilkes' Spirit of the Times* described the intimidating coolness of James Creighton, who "stood at his post, carelessly tossing the ball in the air. The first ball thrown to the bat went like a bullet, the stroke of the bat being made simultaneously with the ball entering the catcher's hands. The batter

Creighton would menacingly toss the ball in the air while the opposing batter steeled himself to face Creighton's blinding fastball.

had never [seen] such a [pitch]; and three misses followed." The Excelsiors won by 45 runs, 51–6, but "the game closed with the conviction on the part of the Baltimore club that the Brooklyn nine could have made more runs had they desired it."

The Excelsiors took the Sunday night train to Philadelphia, where, in front of 1,500 spectators, they played a Monday afternoon game against a team made up of the better players from several Philadelphia clubs. Philadelphia was second in population to New York City and had a lively sports scene; it remained the capital of American cricket for a century. A handful of Philadelphia town ball clubs had already begun to switch over to baseball, as had some talented cricketers, so it is not surprising that the Excelsiors had a tougher time than in Baltimore. Behind ex-New York Knickerbocker pitcher and cricket bowler Richard Stevens, and future baseball stars Wes Fisler and Nate Berkenstock, the Philadelphia "Picked Nine" lost, 15–4. The score tells the story: this game was decided not by hitting but by Philadelphia's inability to handle James Creighton. A reporter wrote that "special wonder" was excited in the crowd by "the daring, almost reckless catching of Leggett, and the swift, even pitching of Creighton." That evening, Colonel Thomas Fitzgerald hosted a dinner for the New Yorkers at Schuylkill Falls, then outside the city. A transplanted New Yorker who had grown up playing baseball in the 1820s in Manhattan's City Hall Park, Fitzgerald was a wealthy newspaper publisher and cofounder of the great Athletic Club. He was all in on persuading Philadelphians to convert to the New York game. The Excelsiors packed sandwiches and took the 11 o'clock night train home.

The outbreak of the Civil War in the spring of 1861 postponed the Excelsiors' planned trips to Boston and Washington, DC. In July of 1862, the Excelsiors were able to accept their invitation to play two games on Boston Common.

In the decades before the Civil War, there were dozens of clubs in and around Boston that played "roundball," which was another name for the Massachusetts game. This was a bat-and-ball game with bases (of a sort) that was similar to town ball, rounders and cricket. Without going into detail about games that have been extinct for 150 years, baseball is different from all other bat-and-ball games in three fundamental ways: three men out, all out in an inning; foul territory; and the distinction between reaching base and scoring a run. Baseball has all three; the others have none. Like baseball, the Massachusetts game was evolving and becoming more organized in the late 1850s. Unlike baseball, it lacked ambition. When Bostonians formed a governing body in 1858, they chose to call it the "*Massachusetts* Association of Base Ball Players." The New York clubs took the aspirational name of the "*National* Association of Base Ball Players." This was a bold statement, considering that the association did not have a single member outside of a 50-mile radius of New York City Hall. Another difference was that when baseball came to conquer Boston and Philadelphia, the enemy had already breeched the gates. In the 1840s, 1850s and 1860s, baseball travelled *from* New York, but no town ball or Massachusetts game club was founded *in* New York. In 1857 a member of New York City's Gotham Club who had moved to Boston for work cofounded the Tri-Mountains, Boston's first club that played by New York baseball rules. In 1858, the Tri-Mountains publicly resigned from the Massachusetts Association because they "preferred to play the New York game."

Three years before James Creighton and the Excelsiors came to town, the Tri-Mountains played Boston's first interclub baseball game. They faced a Maine club, the Portlands, on the Common. Closely connected to New York City and Brooklyn through the shipbuilding industry, southern Maine played New York-style baseball. A young Boston athlete named James D'Wolf Lovett was there. In his 1906 memoir, he compares his fellow Massachusetts game players encountering baseball for the first time to casual attendees pulled into a religious revival meeting.

> This match was attended by many ball players, local and otherwise, who were curious to see what the new thing was like, and who looked on with a dignified toleration befitting those who "guessed" that the old game was good enough for them. But some who came to scoff remained to pray. It was evident that this new type was "catching" and that many present were in that condition when they are said to "take things." There were points about the new game which appealed to

> them. The pitching, instead of swift throwing, looked easy to hit, and the pitcher stood off so far, and then there was no danger of getting plugged with the ball while running bases; and the ball was so lively and could be batted so far! Yes, decidedly, there were points about this new game which pleased many who had never played ball before, and who thought that they would like to try it....

It is ironic that one of baseball's original selling points was its slow, easy pitching. Massachusetts game pitchers did not "pitch;" they threw overhand and fast like modern baseball pitchers, but from much closer to the batter. Another was baseball's elastic ball, which could be swatted astounding distances. In 1859 the Bowdoin Club had switched to baseball, which made two Boston clubs playing the New York game. When the Excelsiors came to town in 1862, the Massachusetts game was not the only game in town, but it was vigorous and still the hometown favorite.

In July of 1862, the Excelsiors took the boat to Fall River, Massachusetts and changed to a train to Boston. On July 10th, they faced the Bowdoin Club on Boston Common. Once again, James D'Wolf Lovett tells us what happened.

> [The Excelsiors] were in their prime at this time and, being the first New York club to visit Boston, created much excitement...Ball players from all parts of New England came to see them play, and our eyes were opened to many things. They beat the Bowdoins, 41 to 15. Much good-natured chaff was passed back and forth between [Bowdoins player and president] John Lowell and Joe Leggett in this game, which made fun for everybody. Once when the latter was at the bat, he motioned to John, who was then playing center field, to go back a little further; John backed off about ten feet, upon which Leggett sung out, "A little further, still, John," and the latter, laughing, backed away another ten feet, whereupon Leggett struck a ball and sent it flying over John's head for a home run, amidst shouts of laughter from the crowd. It was certainly a privilege to have seen Jim Creighton pitch and Joe Leggett catch him. Creighton was at this time but sixteen years old [sic:

> he was actually 21]! And yet nobody had ever approached him in speed and accuracy of delivery.

Lovett then gives a careful description of Creighton's pitching delivery, which Lovett studied and attempted to copy. It refutes the idea that James Creighton was illegally "throwing." What Lovett calls Creighton's "peculiar wrist movement" is the upward flip of the hand and fingers that we discussed in the previous chapter of this book, not the "disguised wrist throw" that Creighton was posthumously—and falsely—accused of using. Note that Lovett says that he imitated Creighton in keeping his elbow entirely straight throughout.

> Creighton had a great influence upon my success as a pitcher. I noted him very carefully and found that his speed was not due to mere physical strength, but that this latter was supplemented by a very long arm and a peculiar wrist movement, very quick and "snappy"—so much so that he was accused of underhand throwing, as I was, afterwards; and I have only to say that if a throw can be accomplished with a perfectly rigid elbow-joint, then he and I were both guilty; but a throw was never proven and neither of us was ever ruled out.

The next day the Excelsiors defeated a composite nine made from the Tri-Mountains and the Lowell Club, 39–13.

Thanks in large part to James Creighton's star power, before the end of the 1860s baseball was king in Boston and Philadelphia, as it soon would be everywhere else. Though cricket was locally popular and boosted by the press, by then it was obvious that it was never going to be the favorite pastime of anyone other than English expatriates and the Philadelphia elite. Other baseball clubs emulated the Excelsiors' tours of 1860 and 1862. In the middle and late 1860s, eastern powerhouses like the Atlantics, Eckfords, Athletics and Nationals made yearly expeditions by ship and railroad, mostly to the Midwest. They routinely demolished the local talent in places like St. Louis, Cincinnati and Chicago. Until 1869 baseball was still an amateur sport, but nothing happens in America without someone trying to make a buck from it. The trips paid for themselves, thanks to ticket sales and—over the loud protests of Henry Chadwick and the deafening silence of the rest of the baseball establishment—gambling. Gambling was a threat to baseball's respectability because the Protestant middle classes considered it immoral. In 1868 the Atlantics and their "outside friends"—an entourage of gamblers, bookmakers, prizefighters and underworld figures—had a wild fistfight with a gang of toughs on a train crossing upstate New York. Creighton, Leggett and the boys had paid their own way, but on later tours players and backers of other clubs were rumored to have bet on their own games; there was talk of games being dumped and scores manipulated to work the betting odds. The 1867 Washington Nationals tour was marred by rumors of game fixing. Regardless, these tours contributed to the cause by showcasing the game's best clubs and players, and by inspiring envy. Tired of losing, Midwesterners decided to hire ringers from Brooklyn and the East. This is how the Cincinnati Red Stockings went from sub-mediocrity to the best team in the country in two years. The combination of imported mercenaries and rising homegrown talent brought a degree of regional parity to baseball. Without the 1860s tours and their after-effects, it is hard to imagine how the first national professional baseball leagues of the 1870s would have succeeded.

THE BATTLE OF BROOKLYN

In the 1860 championship series, for the first time in baseball history, fans became the story, and not in a good way.

It is hard to believe how blind the men who ran amateur baseball were to the inevitability of baseball becoming popular entertainment. For decades, almost nobody watched a baseball game. In the 1840s and early 1850s, a crowd of more than fifty made people wonder why. As baseball drew larger and larger crowds in the late 1850s and 1860s, spectators turned into fans. Fandom meant public interest and money. The first baseball game for which tickets were sold was game one of the Fashion Course Series in 1858, but that was an accident, not a plan. The purpose of charging admission was to pay for damage to the racetrack that hosted the series. Only four years later, a Brooklyn entrepreneur — not a baseball man — built the first enclosed baseball park as a profit-making venture, offered to let amateur clubs use it for free, and sold tickets.

Fandom also fanned the growth of gambling. This was another trend that the baseball establishment and most of its allies in the press dealt with by not dealing with it. Henry Chadwick, baseball's most influential journalist — and its unofficial conscience — campaigned fiercely to keep gambling at arm's length from baseball. He was a voice crying out in the wilderness. Other writers reported the betting line as matter-of-factly as they reported the statistics and the scores. In 1860, one newspaper wrote of witnessing open gambling at a game between two unnamed clubs in New York. "Offers of bets were freely taken," it said, "and even the scorers were not free from the contagion. We are also told that some of the players had large amounts of money staked on the results.... We have heard...rumors that certain parties had sold this or that match — meaning that they were rewarded to play badly." We modern sports fans know what that means.

Reading the newspapers from year to year, we can trace the arrival and growth of the fan. At game one of the Fashion Course Series, reported the *New-York Tribune*, the crowd was annoyed by a lone heckler, who was yelling comments to the players on the field. A woman rose and asked, "Are you a ballplayer, too?" This effectively shamed the offender into silence. This tells us that most of the crowd in 1858 were naive spectators, not baseball fans. They were there to watch, not to root. An exchange like this would not happen at a major-league ballpark today because all modern baseball spectators are fans — many of us grew up playing it and all of us grew up watching it — and we feel entitled to voice our opinions as loudly as we please. Baseball fans see themselves as part of the action, not as the studio audience. A comment like that of the anonymous woman in 1858 is as unthinkable today as fans wearing team baseball caps and team jerseys would have been in the mid-nineteenth century.

By 1860, crowds of four figures at big baseball games had become ordinary. On July 28, 1860, the Excelsiors played against the Stars in Red Hook. The Brooklyn *Daily Eagle* felt it necessary to explain why the "number present...was very small, not numbering over 500." The reason was a competing attraction, the arrival that afternoon in New York Harbor of the *Great Eastern*, the world's largest ship. Only a few years earlier, a crowd as large as 500 at a baseball game would have provoked amazement. The biggest games of 1860 drew crowds twenty or thirty times that size. More significant than their numbers, these crowds were full of fans who were rooting for their teams. We know this from how they behaved — or misbehaved.

The climax of the 1860 season was the three-game series between the Atlantics and Excelsiors. The club that won two would be the champion (unless the winner was upset by the Eckfords, which almost happened). "For a month or more," wrote the Brooklyn *Daily Eagle*, "the baseball public has been alive with interest concerning this great match." The cosmos itself seemed to be paying attention. On July 18th, the day before the series opener, the moon partially eclipsed the sun, casting an unnatural early darkness over Brooklyn. Meteorological events like this one were more magical and more frightening in the days before they could be forecast like the weather.

On July 19th, the Atlantics came to Red Hook to play the first game of the series. It was the hottest day of the summer. The New York *Atlas* compared the Excelsiors grounds to "the Desert of Sahara, one of the most uncomfortable spots that could be found on the globe." Considering the humidity in Brooklyn that day, the Sahara might have been less uncomfortable. That did not stop a sweaty crowd of thousands from filling up every square foot of foul territory, forcing latecomers to perch on nearby buildings and in the masts and rigging of ships docked in the Gowanus. There were no precise attendance counts in the 1860s, but this was said to be the largest baseball crowd ever, even larger than those at the Fashion Course Series two years earlier. It was a home game for the Excelsiors, but most of the crowd — like most of Brooklyn — was rooting for the Atlantics. According to the *Daily*

Eagle, pregame betting odds stood 10 to 8 on the Atlantic Club. The weekly *Spirit of the Times* reported that "a large amount of money was depending, as both clubs have strong admirers."

The Excelsiors came to Red Hook that day with a plan. One year to the day after James Creighton made his first pitching appearance, they executed that plan. The hitters hit. Joe Leggett directed the defense and stopped Creighton's pitches. Reynolds, Pearsall and Holder were outstanding in the field. Creighton mixed his trademark knee-high lightning with a baffling rising curve. The first three Atlantics struck out or popped up. For the next three hours, Creighton was as close to unhittable as a pitcher could be in baseball in 1860. "To Creighton," said the *New York Times* "...must be awarded the highest praise, his pitching being the theme of universal commendation both for its swiftness and regularity. He has well earned the reputation of the most effective pitcher in this region." The *Atlas* said, simply, "The Atlantics could not bat Creighton's balls." Creighton blanked the heavy-hitting Atlantics in six out of the nine innings; the Atlantics managed more than a single run only in the seventh, when they scored two. Three Atlantics batters struck out; eleven were put out on foul tips caught by Leggett. The final score was 23–4. It was never close. "The result," reported the *Daily Eagle*, "was an entire disappointment to the large crowd in attendance, judging from their moving away like a solemn funeral procession after the game was over." If you are a baseball fan, you have been there.

The next day startled New Yorkers witnessed another mysterious communication from the heavens. A train of giant fireballs, later discovered to have been a rare meteor procession, streaked slowly across the sky over southern New York. Like James Creighton's pitching, this so-called "Great Meteor" provoked fear and awe. It inspired a painting by Frederic Edwin Church and a poem by Walt Whitman. In the year 44 BC, Romans had witnessed a similar meteorological phenomenon and decided that it signified the deification of another popular hero with the initials J. C.—the assassinated Julius Caesar. Caesar, of course, was a left-hander.

The two teams met again on August 9th. The weather was still hot and sticky, but a new record-setting crowd, perhaps as large as 15,000, massed on the Atlantics' grounds in Bedford. The Brooklyn *Daily Eagle* painted the pregame picture.

> From one to three o'clock, yesterday afternoon, the avenues leading to the Atlantic ball ground in Bedford, were thronged with pedestrians, *en route* to witness the great match...during that time it was a difficult matter to obtain standing room on either the Myrtle avenue or Fulton Avenue cars, so crowded were they.... On arriving at the ground, the scene itself was at once novel and picturesque. The space of ground allotted to the players was encircled by a line of vehicles of every description from the carriage and pair of the wealthy citizen to the peddler's cart with its sorry nag.... Outside the circle one would have supposed some great fair was in progress, so numerous were the various itinerant tradesmen and vendors of eatables and drinkables. Fancy colored tents headed the field, and in some King Lager held his levee, his court being pretty well filled with thirsty worshippers, and in others his potent rival, King Alcohol... emitted flashes of "Jersey Lightning" [100-proof apple brandy].

"The friends of both parties were out in force," said the *Times*, "and any success on either side was greeted with loud applause, the Atlantic throats being in the ascendancy." For almost two hours, game two looked like *déjà vu* all over again. Creighton was Creighton, and the score was 11–0 Excelsiors going into the bottom of the fourth inning. After Joe Leggett uncharacteristically allowed several pitches to get by him, the Atlantics rallied and began to chip away at the deficit. They scored two in the fourth, one in the fifth and three in the sixth to narrow the Excelsiors' lead to 12–6.

Then came the unlikeliest inning in Amateur Era baseball history, an inning that the Atlantics would always celebrate as their "lucky seventh." The New York *Atlas* wrote, "we are somewhat at a loss for terms to describe the batting of the Atlantics in this innings. To say it was splendid seems tame, certain it has never been surpassed in the annals of the game." The Atlantics batted around, every man but one crossing the plate at least once. When it was over, they had scored nine runs to go ahead, 15–12. Utterly gassed after throwing 236 pitches in the August heat, James Creighton switched positions with left fielder Russell. It was first time—and the only time—he was replaced as a pitcher for ineffectiveness. The drama, however, was not over. Ed Russell somehow got the Atlantics out in the eighth and ninth, while the Excelsiors launched their own desperate comeback. They scored a run in the eighth and another in the ninth to cut the Atlantics' lead down to one run, but with two outs catcher Dickey Pearce ended the game by throwing out Joe Leggett at second. The Atlantics won 15–14. The championship of 1860 would be decided by a third game.

Or maybe not.

Game three was set for Thursday, August 23rd, at a neutral site with lots of room for spectators and access to public transit, the home field of Williamsburg's Putnam Club. In the days leading up to the game, there was an ominous feeling in the air. Rumors circulated that the Excelsiors "would not be allowed to win in a close contest"—whatever that meant. There were noticeably fewer women at the game than usual, as if they could smell trouble. Creighton pitched for the Excelsiors, Mattie O'Brien for the Atlantics. The game began at 3:35 PM, a bit late, in front of a crowd estimated by the *New York Clipper* at twelve thousand people. Among them were delegations of ballplayers from Albany, Troy, Buffalo and Rochester—returning the visits of the Excelsiors earlier that summer—as well as from Boston, Philadelphia and Baltimore.

The next day baseball fans opened up their paper, turned to the sports page and spat out their morning coffee. "THE GAME BROKEN UP BY ROWDIES" was the headline. The Excelsiors were batting with two out in the bottom of the sixth, leading 8–6—an unusually low score—when Captain Leggett took his team off the field, ending the game. He explained that he had had enough of the fans' verbal abuse of his club, and that in the previous inning he had warned the umpire and the Atlantics that the Excelsiors would quit if it continued. After the game, Umpire Thorn issued a somewhat

Talmudic statement that said, "My decision is that the game was won by neither party.... But, as the stoppage of the game was not by mutual consent, I must, according to the rules, decide that the party refusing to play, forfeits ..." As for the game itself, there is not much to tell. The Atlantics scored one run in the first, two in the second, one in the third and two in the fifth. The Excelsiors scored five in the first inning, one in the third and two in the fourth. In the fifth inning, the umpire called Atlantics center fielder Archie McMahon out after he overran third base and was tagged. McMahon made it clear that he thought he was safe; the fans were too far away to see anything, but of course they booed the call. In an ordinary game, this would have been unremarkable. The same cannot be said for the way the game ended. The Atlantics won 6–8 and backed into the championship of baseball. A month later, at a post-game banquet in Baltimore, the president of the host club toasted the visitors as "the champion club of the United States." The always witty Dr. Jones of the Brooklyn Excelsiors "begged to be excused from receiving the compliment."

In the days and weeks following this fiasco, the press closed ranks behind the Excelsiors. Every paper that covered sports blamed the Atlantics and their fans for—whatever it was that had happened. The national weekly, *Porter's Spirit of the Times*, wrote that the game was "not completed on account of the rowdy demonstrations made by some of the spectators...the crowd of roughs who backed the Atlantic Club considered that the umpire, Mr. Thorn of the Empire Club, gave some decisions that did injustice to their side, whereupon they commenced annoying the Umpire and the Excelsior nine with insulting and blackguard [i.e., abusive] epithets." *Porter's* went on to complain that "Both clubs this summer have been followed by crowds of dirty-faced roughs and half-grown ragged-tailed boys, who have made it very disagreeable for decent spectators to witness the games." Pearl-clutching commentators lamented the crowd's "rowdyism," "hooting," "groaning," "insults," "loud comments," and "yelling."

Henry Chadwick did not hold the Atlantics responsible, nor did he attribute the crowd's behavior to the partisan passion of fans. Instead, he pointed his finger at gambling. "If the admirers of this manly pastime desire its future welfare," he wrote, 'they should at once proceed to adopt stringent rules...*against betting on the result of the matches played*, for it was unquestionably a regard for their pockets alone that led the majority of those particularly interested in the affair, to act in the blackguard manner they did...the result of the contest being a drawn game, *all bets being off* [italics Chadwick's]."

History has swallowed Chadwick's version whole. You can find it today if you consult any baseball history source. There are, however, grounds for skepticism. It may be true that a significant portion of the crowd had bets down on the Atlantics, and it is plausible that some of those who had bet were worried—or even angry—that the Excelsiors might hold onto their small lead and that they would lose their money. But what exactly did these supposedly nervous, angry bettors do to chase the Excelsiors off the field? Chadwick implies that gamblers had intentionally provoked the forfeit to protect the money that they had bet. How did they control an allegedly out-of-control crowd of thousands? And why? When the Excelsiors walked off the field, the Atlantics were mounting a comeback, just as they had in game two, and the Excelsiors lead had shrunk from 8–4 to 8–6. (In game two there was no fan misbehavior with the Excelsiors leading 11–2 and the Atlantics five innings away from a humiliating sweep). In game three, behind by two runs and closing with at least six outs left, you would expect Atlantics fans to be hopeful, not hostile.

There is zero evidence that the Excelsiors were in any physical danger. The reporters who were there had a clear pro-Excelsiors bias and no motive to minimize the behavior of the crowd. On the contrary, they exaggerated it; yet not one of them alleges a single act of physical violence or threat of violence. There are no reports, for example, of fans throwing anything or charging onto the field—only cheering, booing and rough language. An uncontradicted published account from a man who was in the stands that day stated that no one tried to cross the rope that separated the crowd from the playing field. When people run out of facts, they fall back on *ad hominem* reasoning, which is what the newspapers in 1860 did. They argued that if a great guy like Joe Leggett took his team off the field, then he must have had a good reason. "Expressions of dissent," wrote Chadwick, "became so decided, and symptoms of bad feeling began to manifest itself to such a degree, that the Captain of the Excelsior nine, Mr. Leggett, than whom a fairer, more manly, or more gentlemanly player does not exist, ordered his men to pick up their bats and retire from the field."

This argument would be weak enough on its own. But the truth is that Joe Leggett was no gentleman.

In the 1860s, the position of catcher in baseball required a degree of physical courage that we can barely imagine. Catchers had no mitts, face masks, shin guards or chest protectors. The only thing stopping a pitched ball from bounding away from the field, while runners circled the bases, was the catcher's unpadded body. Pitchers of that time were rarely taken out of a game, but catchers were commonly removed with black eyes, broken noses or fractured fingers. When the count reached two strikes, an aggressive catcher would move up behind the batter and spread out his bare hands, risking his health in order to catch a foul tip. This was Leggett's forte. In his 1868 baseball instructional Henry Chadwick referred to this technique as "taking balls sharp off the bat, à la Joe Leggett..." There is no questioning Joe Leggett's toughness and physical courage. He was a valued teammate. Older than most of the Excelsiors, Joe Leggett was looked up to as a father figure. Well respected in baseball generally, he was elected vice president of baseball's governing body, the National Association of Base Ball Players, in 1862. But off the field, Leggett was a different person.

Joseph Bowne Leggett was born in 1828 in Stillwater, a town in Saratoga County in upstate New York. He moved to Brooklyn as a young man to work in the family wholesale grocery business. He became a volunteer fireman with the baseball-playing Pacific Engine Company #14 on Love Lane in Brooklyn Heights. Engine Company #14 was also a kind of family business. Leggett, his cousin James Leggett and another relative, Isaac Leggett, all served terms as foreman. James Leggett later became president of the Brooklyn Fire Department.

In 1867 the 39-year-old Joseph Leggett married a much younger Englishwoman named Alice Marks; they had three children.

Like other star athletes then and now, Leggett lived off his celebrity. During his playing career, he held day jobs in institutions connected to the powerful men behind the Excelsiors, but as an employee he had a short shelf life. Leggett was repeatedly caught stealing or embezzling and then fired, transferred or allowed to resign. He simply could not keep his hand out of the till. His thefts were haphazard, opportunistic—and pathetic. His family stood by him, and his old friends and teammates gave him one second chance after another. A likely explanation is that he was personally likeable, that people felt sorry for him because of some underlying vice, or both. Being a sports hero probably did not hurt. In 1859 Leggett was employed by Brooklyn's Mercantile Library Association, a pet charity of the wealthy, where he was caught trying to rig an officers' election, causing a scandal. During the Civil War, army quartermasters were responsible for purchasing and distributing food and essential supplies for military units. They handled a lot of cash. Someone thought it was a good idea to appoint Leggett as quartermaster of the Brooklyn-based Thirteenth New York State Militia. That someone was the commanding officer of the Thirteenth NYSM, Colonel John Woodward, a fellow member of the Excelsior baseball club. In an 1861 letter from the front, Woodward called Leggett, "the very best fellow in the entire universe." Allegations by soldiers that Leggett sold provisions meant for his regiment, replaced them with cheaper products and pocketed the difference, were hushed up.

The Excelsiors' powerful backers continued to take care of Leggett after he was finished as a player. In 1869 he was put in charge of the Widows and Orphans Fund of the Brooklyn Fire Department. Three years later, it was discovered that he had failed to deposit nearly $3,000 raised by a charity ball. "The very best fellow in the entire universe" literally robbed widows and orphans. Leggett's boss, a fellow ex-firefighter from Engine Company #14, said he had dropped the matter because Leggett promised to pay the money back, which he didn't. When this came out, Leggett was forced to resign. Leggett's increasingly shady résumé did not prevent the Brooklyn Police Department, (which had a history of hiring Excelsiors and other ballplayers), from giving him a clerkship in the Excise Bureau, which issued liquor licenses. This job also involved handling large sums of cash. In 1877 it emerged that Leggett had collected several thousand dollars in application fees from bar owners who never got their licenses. Leggett did not wait to be fired. On January 4, 1878, a Brooklyn newspaper reported,

> Joe Leggett, the runaway clerk of the Excise Bureau, is still wanted at Police Headquarters. His whereabouts is a mystery. In consequence of his sudden and improvident departure his wife was obligated a few days before New Year's to give up her residence in Monroe Street, and she and her children are now boarding with friends.... Leggett's best friends are loud in their denunciation of his misconduct, and loud in their praise of his wife's fortitude under crushing trial.

Leggett left New York around Christmastime 1877, abandoned his wife and children, and disappeared. In Leggett's time men on the run often went west. Facing homelessness, Alice Leggett and her children were taken in temporarily by Joseph Leggett's cousin James, who lived in Rockland County, New York. For most of the next twenty years, Alice Leggett supported the family by herself, working as a governess, teacher and matron of a home for unwed mothers. She said that she never saw her husband again.

In 1899 Alice retired and applied for a military widow's pension. She claimed not to have heard from him or about him since 1882, but there is reason to think that Leggett's new name and location may have been an open secret in the baseball world. It also seems that he even made occasional trips to Brooklyn. In 1885, Henry Chadwick wrote that he saw Leggett "frequently about town." In another column Chadwick tells of running into Leggett coming out of Brooklyn City Hall. In 1889 Henry Chadwick reminisced in print about the glory days of the old Excelsiors. "Ed Russell, Asa Brainard and Tom Reynolds are dead and gone," he wrote, "Pearsall is a doctor in the South...Harry Polhemus is one of Brooklyn's society men and a millionaire; John Whiting is in business in this city, and his brother Charley also, I believe, while Joe Leggett is—well, I will be silent for old times' sake." The most interesting part of that quotation is Chadwick's choice of the present tense, especially in light of what I found when I located the original paper files on Mrs. Leggett's pension application. Joe Leggett was indeed alive in 1889. The information in these files goes a long way toward solving the mystery of where Leggett went in 1877 and why. The surprise is that it also sheds new light on Joe Leggett's odd behavior during the Atlantics series of 1860.

The press backed Leggett and the Excelsiors, but there was some dissent from the narrative that the crowd's disorderly behavior—encouraged, or at least not discouraged, by Atlantics players—justified stopping game three of the 1860 championship series. Two days after the game, umpire Thorn issued a statement. "I must say," it read, "that I heard no disputing of the decisions on their part that an umpire [could] take umbrage at, while the playing was going on. On the part of the outsiders, I have nothing to say—the gentlemen who were present can judge for themselves. I paid no attention to what was said outside the game. The first intimation that I had of the stoppage of the game was an exclamation [by Leggett] that if the outsiders did not stop blackguarding them and the umpire, he would call in his men, throw up the game, and give the ball to the Atlantics. On the strength of this assertion—as there did not appear to be any cessation of the noise—Mr. Leggett fulfilled his word, and the play was stopped without any action of mine in the matter, other than stating to Mr. Leggett that it made no difference to me how many remarks or how much noise there was made, so far as I was concerned..."

An anonymous letter sent to *Porter's Spirit of the Times* by an eyewitness calling himself "Home Run" argues that there was "not a sufficient *cause* for the captain of the Excelsior nine to withdraw his men from the field, when a game which could only have extended to seven innings was so near its conclusion. The field was clear, the rope was perfect around its entire extent, and every player could exhibit as perfect play as he was capable of. Why should such experienced and able players as the Excelsiors heed or pay any attention to the noisy demonstrations of the rabble?" Another source corroborates the fact that the pace of the game was slow, that it was getting dark, and that the game would have been called after seven innings. This is significant because it means that Leggett pulled his players off the field with two outs in what would have been the next to last inning.

On August 31, Frederick Boughton, president of the Atlantic Club, issued his own public statement. It makes interesting reading for modern baseball fans wondering what all the fuss was about, because it leaves us still wondering.

> In consequence of there being so much comment reflecting on us in regard to our late match with the Excelsior Club, and the press so unanimous in adjudging all the odium consequent upon the abrupt termination of the game on the Atlantic Club and their friends, we think that in simple justice to ourselves and to them we are bound to make a frank record of the affair, and in the confident hope and anticipation that a discerning public will, now that the excitement has in a measure subsided, give our side of the story a fair and just hearing.
>
> In the first place, we used every possible effort to have a "clear field and no favor," and, as in the last game, we feel happy to say that...we succeeded beyond the possibility of doubt. What more can any club do? Can we restrain a burst of applause or indignation emanating from an assemblage of more than 15,000 excited spectators...? He who has witnessed the natural excitement which is ever the attendant of...a regatta, an important trial of speed on the turf, or a match between noted baseball organizations, knows full well that it is an utter impossibility to prevent the crowd from expressing their sentiments in a manner and as audibly as they please.
>
> Mr. Thorn, the umpire on this occasion, was calm, and expressed himself not at all annoyed by the exclamations of the spectators.... Then let us ask what caused [the] abrupt termination? Nothing, in our opinion, judging from the language made use of, but the ungovernable temper of a friend of ours on the other side, who seems to be getting

> exceedingly nervous of late... In conclusion, we must say that no one was more surprised or disappointed at the termination of the game than ourselves. We were confident of victory, and we wish the public to remember that the "Old Atlantics" are used to fighting these exciting battles; and we would recommend to those aspiring to the championship not to be too hasty in leaving the field, as it is a "poor road to travel," and does not lead to that enviable and coveted position.

In other words, fans are part of the game now; and if you cannot stand the heat, then get out of the kitchen.

Boughton's letter contains a clue to the mystery of why the Excelsiors forfeited the championship of 1860. The phrase "the ungovernable temper of a friend of ours on the other side, who seems to be getting exceedingly nervous of late" refers to Joe Leggett. Apparently, Leggett had been acting strangely, noticeably so. It is hard to believe that Leggett could have been rattled by the pressure of the game; Leggett and the Excelsiors had played other big games in front of other big crowds. What was Leggett "nervous" about?

Alice Leggett's 1899 pension application was witnessed by Colonel Frank Jones, an important baseball man who had played with the Excelsiors before the Civil War. Jones went to Washington, DC during the war, joined the National baseball club and built that club into a national power. In Washington in 1866, he had introduced Joe Leggett to Alice Marks; he attended their wedding. Alice Leggett had no trouble proving that her husband had served in the military, but the sticking point was proving that he was dead. She tried the same legal arguments that are used today to have someone declared legally dead absent a corpse—that she had not heard from her husband for 17 years, that they had been happily married, and he had no reason to stop writing to her unless he was no longer alive. She and her in-laws had tried to locate him, she said, and failed. Even if all of this was not exactly true, Alice Leggett did us a favor. If her case had not been weak and an anonymous federal auditor had not held out for better proof, we would not know the second half of Joe Leggett's life story.

When the pension process stalled, Colonel Jones hired a big time DC lawyer to represent Mrs. Leggett. The lawyer sent a private detective to try to find out what had happened to him. The pension file contains the detective's report and depositions from Alice Leggett and various friends, associates and family members. Her depositions are colored by a reluctance to concede that her husband had any reason to go into hiding. If he did not want to be found, of course, this would undercut her argument that his long silence meant that he could be presumed dead. Asked if Joe Leggett had gone on the run to avoid being arrested and prosecuted for embezzlement, she explains that the Chief of the Brooklyn Police told her that they had dropped the matter years earlier. This actually seems to be true. It is backed up by the private detective who concluded, "soldier appears to have been a defaulter when he left in December 1877, but he was not indicted or pursued, and it does not appear that this defalcation had anything to do with his disappearance." Mrs. Leggett testified that she had been corresponding with her husband regularly until he abruptly stopped writing in 1882. As she told it, after Joe Leggett left Brooklyn, he went to Dayton, Ohio and worked on a farm. After that, he was homeless for a time. Later, while Leggett was living under an assumed name in Wyoming, he received mail, addressed to his alias, care of a general store in Cheyenne. Presumably because he did not want her to know that he was using a false name — or why — and because he did not want anyone in Cheyenne to discover his real name, he instructed his wife to address her letters not to his alias or his name but to "JBL."

Asked if Joe Leggett had a problem with alcohol, Alice Leggett first tells the private detective that her husband drank no more than moderately but later changes her story, saying that drinking was his only "fault," and that "it was for this reason that he [decided] to go away and form new associations and start life anew." According to Alice Leggett, her father-in-law told her in the early 1880s that he visited Joe in Wyoming and was happy to see that he was not drinking *and* "had not resumed his old habits." It may be true or partly true that Joe Leggett had a drinking problem, or it may be a red herring. Leggett's friends in the West, not all of whom knew each other, were unanimous in their statements to the private detective that Leggett did not drink. He was, however, careless with money. Mrs. Leggett provides the private detective with a long list of her husband's business failures and bankruptcies in Brooklyn, which repeatedly forced the family to move when Joe Leggett was unable to pay the rent or the mortgage.

In the late 1870s and the 1880s, western states were experiencing a cattle boom. With beef prices rising, ranchers began to move their herds from the Midwest to public land farther west. In places like Wyoming and Colorado, rich grazing land could be leased from the government for almost nothing. Cattlemen could simply sit back, watch their cattle and their bank accounts grow fat—and congratulate themselves on being successful businessmen. This is the origin of several great American family fortunes that are still with us today. Around 1881, Joseph Leggett's father and brother decided to set him up with a cattle ranch, both to help him and as an investment. According to the pension file, Leggett bought the ranch 30 miles outside of Cheyenne with "$800–$1000" of his family's money. He then bought a herd of cattle on credit. Less than a year later, however, he could not make the loan payments and declared bankruptcy. He was forced to sell the ranch, clearing $1500. This may represent a profit on the original investment, but it was not enough, the private investigator writes, "to pay the "debts [that Leggett] owed in Cheyenne." He walked away with nothing.

Of all the ways to go into debt in Cheyenne, Wyoming in the late 1870s, the easiest and most likely was gambling. Gambling was a way of life in both Cheyenne and the West as a whole. A gambling addiction would explain Leggett's lifelong pattern of money problems, bankruptcies, failed businesses, and amateurish acts of stealing. In those days, even the most committed alcoholic or sex addict would have trouble blowing thousands of dollars on booze or prostitutes. People who steal the way Leggett did do so because they need cash right now, because they owe someone. Leggett may also had had a drinking problem—gambling addicts often do—but alcoholism makes no sense as the main driver of Leggett's behavior. You could see him moving out of Brooklyn to escape unhealthy company and to start a new life of sobriety. But he could have done that in New Jersey, and he could have brought his family. It is also hard to see how changing his name (and keeping it a secret from his own wife) would help him stop drinking. Whatever he was running away from, it made Joe Leggett run 1,750 miles, change his name and keep moving, taking great care not to be found. Leggett was running away because he was afraid. This would explain why Henry Chadwick did not want to print in the paper where Joe Leggett was living, and why Leggett abandoned Alice Leggett and his children despite credible testimony that he loved them dearly.

Gambling addicts go into debt. They are forced to borrow money, sometimes from dangerous people. What happens when a gambling addict is a star athlete, who owes more money than he can pay back to someone he has reason to be afraid of? He might have to pay the debt by manipulating a game, say by shaving points or losing intentionally. We cannot prove that Joe Leggett was in this predicament, but it fits the known facts better than the explanation we have been given, or any other explanation.

Could Joe Leggett have been trying to throw the championship series against the Atlantics? We have no idea if he was acting alone, but as catcher and field captain of the Excelsiors, he could sabotage his team to some extent by himself by allowing passed balls at critical times, calling the wrong fielder on defensive plays, calling the wrong pitch, or making base running mistakes. There was nothing Leggett could have done to lose game one, but that was only one game. Clearly playing to win, James Creighton was utterly dominant in game one and held the Atlantics to four runs. The only way for the Excelsiors to throw this game would have been to have the entire lineup cooperate to score no more than three runs without making it obvious, which would have been close to impossible.

In game two, Creighton was just as good through the first three innings and the Excelsiors led, 8–0. The Atlantics' comeback began in the fourth inning, when they scored two runs, thanks, according to the *New York Times*, to "two or three passed balls" by Leggett. Leggett helped the Atlantics in a later inning with another multiple-passed ball inning. Two multiple-passed ball innings in the same game was something that had never happened before in Leggett's career. Passed balls were rampant in baseball at that time—double figures were not unusual, but Joe Leggett was the best catcher in baseball at preventing them. His passed ball totals were normally in the low single digits. Historian Tom Shieber added up the number of passed balls in all of Joe Leggett's games in 1860 for which we have data and compared them to the number for the opposing catcher.

	Passed Balls by Leggett	Passed Balls by Opposing Catcher
	2	6
	0	10
	1	5
	1	10
	1	9
	5	11
	1	9
	1	22
	4	6
	4	6
	9	7
	3	1
	1	2
	2	11
	1	6
	3	6
	4	3
TOTAL:	43	130

This chart speaks for itself, but one line stands out. In game two Leggett allowed nine passed balls—his highest total of the season and almost twice his second-highest total.

Then there is the Atlantics' "lucky seventh." Reading the play-by-play in the papers, we cannot accurately judge the quality of the hits made by the Atlantics. We might read, for example, "Pearce hit a good bounding ball to left field." Was this a clean single or a routine grounder that the shortstop or third baseman should have had? There is no way to tell. Another problem is that scorers in 1860 did not record whether runs were earned or unearned. The meticulous Henry Chadwick, who kept his own scoresheets, later wrote about this famous inning that the Atlantics "punished Creighton to the tune of nine scored runs, five of which were earned." If four of the runs scored because of errors, perhaps that explains why the Atlantics called their own seventh inning rally not clutch or heroic — but "lucky." The game story in *Wilkes' Spirit of the Times* contains a telling detail about this inning. After the Atlantics had scored six runs and tied it up, 12–12, "Leggett and Creighton had a moment's consultation. 'Joe' said there was something the matter, and Creighton asked, 'What is it?'" This is awkwardly written, but it appears to be saying that in the middle of the disastrous seventh inning, Creighton asked Leggett what was wrong with him. After this, "Leggett returned to his post." This was followed by a passed ball by Leggett on which Mattie O'Brien "made two bases." Later in the inning, another run scored on another Leggett passed ball.

The ending of game two also gives off a bad odor. Trailing 15–12 after seven, the Excelsiors scored a run in the eighth to make it 15–13. In the ninth inning, with Brainard on third and two outs, Joe Leggett singled to center to bring the Excelsiors to within one run of tying the game. When catcher Dickey Pearce muffed a pitch by Mattie O'Brien, Leggett took off for second but was tagged out to end the game after overrunning the base. Leggett's terrible defense in game two was highly unusual. So was Creighton's mid-inning conversation with him. Should we be suspicious about how Leggett made the final out? In modern baseball, the answer would be no, because a runner is so much more likely to score from second with two outs than from first. This is why second and third are called "scoring position." Taking a chance to advance from first to second can be a good play. But this was not true in baseball as played in 1860. Passed balls were so common that when a runner reached first, games tended to grind to a halt. Batters would keep the bat on their shoulder, letting dozens of hittable pitches go by and refusing to swing until the baserunner moved up. This was the reason for the 1858 rule change that allowed umpires to call warning strikes if batters repeatedly refused to offer at good pitches.

Consider Joe Leggett's state of mind going into the third and deciding game. He has to find a way to lose. He cannot make Creighton pitch badly, and passed balls only help the opposition if there are enough runners on base. His plan to throw the game may have involved somehow making sure that the Excelsiors scored as few runs as possible, counting on the Atlantics bats to do something against Creighton. If so, that plan is not working. The Excelsiors are leading 8–6 in the top of the sixth, and the clock is ticking. It's getting dark and it looks like the game will be called after seven. Leggett is desperate. He has run out of ways to lose, but he then he has an idea. As team captain, he can order his men off the field, using a pretext. They would lose by forfeit.

The Excelsiors' unlikely loss raised a few eyebrows at the time. *Wilkes' Spirit of the Times* felt it necessary to defend the club in print. "The idle rumors spread by some of the disappointed bettors," it wrote, "that there was 'backing and filling' on the part of the Excelsiors, are simply ridiculous. The character of the men engaged on both sides is a sufficient guarantee—if any were needed—to everyone, that the game was played right on the square. We watched the whole proceedings most attentively; and we fancy, from our long experience in such matters, we could have easily detected any departure from the right course on either side." This kind of defense is less than comforting. A few years later, Henry Chadwick's support of Joe Leggett and the Excelsiors had weakened considerably. This is what he wrote in 1866:

> The game was nearly half concluded...when some of the outside rabble made use, so it is said, of obscene language to some of the Excelsior players. Had no notice been taken thereof it perhaps would have ended.... Let the difficulty be what it may, or censure rest where it belonged, the game was stopped by Mr. Leggett. The umpire called for the game to go on, but the Excelsiors said no and wanted to give the ball

to the Atlantics. Mr. Mattie O'Brien refused to accept it, and here the matter rested. That certain players had money on the game, there is no doubt, and deep regret was felt that the game was not played out.

Wait, what? "Certain players" had money on the game?

If Henry Chadwick knew or suspected what Leggett had done and why, it would explain why in 1860 he blamed gambling for what happened in game three, without giving a believable reason why. He knew that gambling was to blame, but he could not tell the whole truth. To write that one of the game's greatest heroes was trying to throw the championship for gamblers would be too damaging to the sport that he loved and spent most of his life working to promote and protect. Why was Joe Leggett "exceedingly nervous" on August 23rd, 1860? He was worried that he might win.

This image was published by Frank Leslie's Illustrated Newspaper *in 1865 — three years after James Creighton's death. The Excelsiors star looks down upon the sport he helped create as if from the next world.*

8 WHAT KILLED J.C.?

FIFTY-THOUSAND MEN young men were killed in the Civil War in 1862, but no one expected to encounter death in the sports section. On October 19th the news broke that baseball's greatest star had lost his life. The next day, James Creighton's 21-year-old body was laid in an expensive rosewood casket with silver mountings, paid for by the Excelsior baseball club. Accompanied by friends, relatives and baseball men, it was carried to his Green-Wood cemetery grave by three teammates from the Excelsiors—Joe Leggett, Harry Polhemus and George Flanley—and one Niagara—David Kent, Creighton's best friend on his first Brooklyn club. The Creighton's family minister, Reverend Dr. North of Brooklyn's York Street Methodist Church (a church that fielded a baseball team), officiated.

The Creighton plot sits on top of Tulip Hill, which at 200 feet above sea level gives a panoramic view of New York Harbor, Staten Island and the New Jersey waterfront. Nearby are the Fireman's Memorial, once a tourist attraction; the burial plot of Americus #6, Boss Tweed's volunteer fire company and political power base; and the grave of New York City Volunteer Fire Department chief engineer Harry Howard, the man who thought of having firemen bunk overnight in the firehouse. If you visit James Creighton today—and people do, judging by the old baseballs that appear daily at the foot of Creighton's grave—you will find the first-ever baseball-themed public monument. Creighton's grave inspired others (including that of Henry Chadwick, who is buried nearby in Green-Wood), but its designer had no precedent to follow. It features an eight-foot-high marble stele with carved crossed baseball bats, a baseball cap, a base, a baseball shoe and an open scorebook. Behind the bats is a banner that read, before it eroded into illegibility,

"Excelsior." The four corners of the main section are decorated with upside-down baseball bats. This is a play on upside down torches, which in the iconography of graves represent life after death — as if to suggest that Creighton had ascended to baseball eternity. It is crowned by marble papyrus leaves — an ancient symbol of transition to the afterlife — supporting a marble baseball with the lemon-peel stitching that was used in Creighton's day. The papyrus and baseball mysteriously disappeared in the early twentieth century, but they were restored in 2014 thanks to a gift from journalist and lover of baseball history Keith Olbermann. Green-Wood cemetery is the final resting place of literally hundreds of important early baseball figures, including at least four men who have been called "The Father of Baseball." Whatever James Creighton is doing now, he is doing it in the company of Henry Chadwick, Joseph Jones, Asa Brainard, Jack Chapman, Lewis Wadsworth, Joseph Pinckney, Harry Polhemus, William Van Cott and dozens of other visionaries who gave us our first national sport.

James Creighton was the most famous baseball player who had ever lived when he died a sudden and shocking death. The closest historical comparison is Cleveland shortstop Ray Chapman, who was killed by a pitch in a major league game in 1920. Chapman was popular and his death made national news, but he does not compare in stature to Creighton. Creighton's grave immediately became a pilgrimage site, a phenomenon that has no parallel in baseball or any sport. For years, baseball men travelled to Green-Wood to honor and remember the man who invented pitching and who made the club that made baseball our national sport. In 1866 the Nationals of Washington, DC, came to Brooklyn to play the Excelsiors, "stopping for a few moments at the grave of Creighton, the Mecca of baseball players, the sole relic of the noblest and manliest exponent that the national game has ever had," reported the Brooklyn *Daily Eagle*. "There are few who have not heard of Mr. Creighton as the pitcher *par excellence*." Three years after Creighton's death, the *Eagle* wrote that "Creighton was the only pitcher who never had an equal." That same year, *Frank Leslie's Illustrated Newspaper* ran a huge, two-page portrait of the world of baseball. At the center is a game in progress at the first ballpark, Brooklyn's Union Grounds. All around are small, full-figure portraits of prominent ballplayers. The principal clubs are listed, but they are divided, as baseball was, between the Brooklyn clubs on one side and the New York City (and other non-Brooklyn) clubs on the other. At the center James Creighton, the largest figure, is shrouded in the black crepe of mourning; he gazes down impassively at the sport that owes him so much.

What killed James Creighton? We will not find answers in the obituaries, eulogies and tributes that followed his death. This is a mystery that has gone unsolved for 160 years. We have a solid time of death: Creighton died at home on October 18th, 1862. But that is not when or where whatever killed him happened.

We can safely rule out anything that occurred on the baseball field in 1861. In April of that year the Civil War happened, and baseball went dormant. The Excelsiors did not play any games against other clubs that year and James Creighton did not join the military. Over 95% of the men who served in the Union Army volunteered. Creighton did not, and there was no draft in the Civil War until July of 1863. As the sole provider of support for an aged parent and an unmarried sister, it is doubtful that Creighton would have been drafted, but by then he was ineligible for a different reason. Cricket clubs were more active than baseball clubs during the early years of the war. Creighton had started to play cricket on the side in 1860, and he was still playing cricket when he died two years later.

Journalists have been confused about the exact cause of James Creighton's death since the day after it happened. So have historians. It is usually described as an accident, a traumatic injury that he suffered in a particular game. He tore his [insert name of internal organ] while swinging a cricket bat at an awkward angle and — oops — he died. Other accounts repeat Jack Chapman's story that Creighton was hitting a home run in a baseball game, tore something, and — oops — he died. Both of these scenarios are contradicted by the known medical facts.

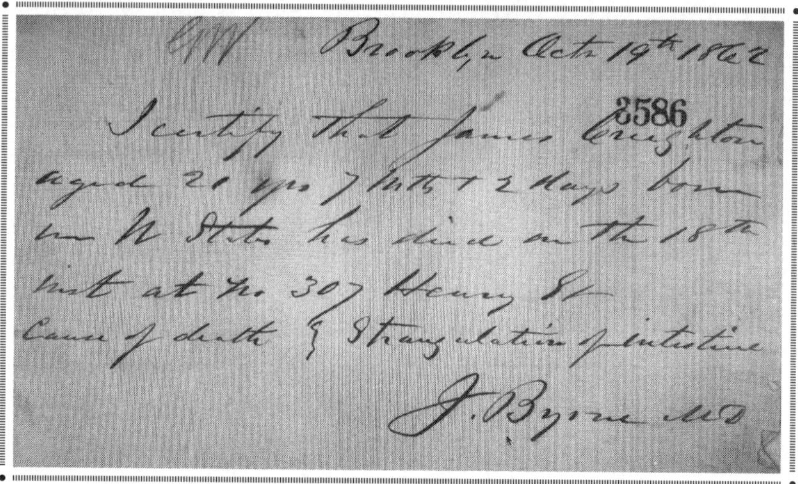

Brooklyn Octr 19th 1862

3586

I certify that James Creighton aged 21 yrs 7 Mths & 2 days born in U States has died on the 18th inst at No. 307 Henry St

Cause of death } Strangulation of intestine

J. Byrne MD

James Creighton's long-misfiled death certificate. It gives his real cause of death — "strangulation of intestine."

James Creighton's death certificate gives the immediate cause of death, but not the whole story. Written in longhand by Dr. John Byrne, who treated him, the certificate reads, "cause of death: strangulation of intestine." Contemporary records at Brooklyn's Green-Wood cemetery say the same thing. A strangulated intestine is the result of a chain of events. It starts at birth with an inherited hernia, which is a gap or weak spot in the abdominal muscle wall. If part of the intestine happens to get caught in the hernia, the blood supply to the intestinal tissue can be cut off and a gangrene infection follows. Inguinal hernias are common among athletes in America today, but they are never fatal because hernias cause symptoms and victims seek medical help well before the crisis point. Modern surgery can easily repair a hernia, and infections are treatable with antibiotics. In James Creighton's time, however, the surgical options were risky and best avoided. A localized infection might be treatable by amputating an extremity or draining an abscess but in a world without antibiotics, an advanced gangrene infection was a death sentence. Dr. Byrne may have tried to free the intestinal tissue and force it back into Creighton's abdomen, which would have been painful, even excruciating, after gangrene set in. At some point Byrne would have realized that there was no hope. James Creighton's body battled a massive internal infection for four agonizing days before he died.

In the mid-nineteenth century both hernias and the risk of a strangulated intestine were well understood by doctors. Creighton would have been getting medical treatment—probably for years—and he would have been wearing a truss to protect the hernia, but he lived and played with pain and most likely with the knowledge that he might develop a strangulated intestine.

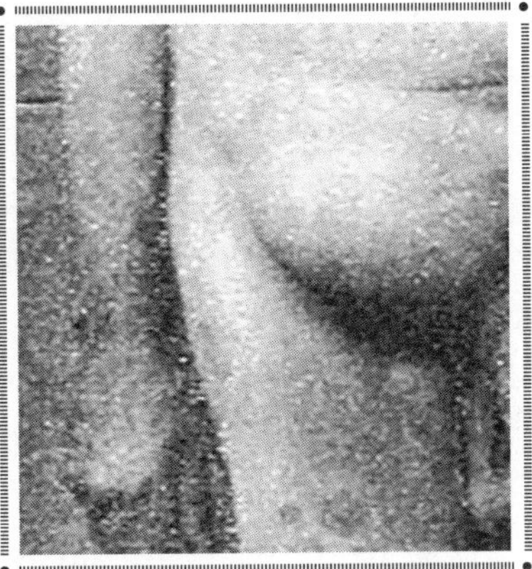

Creighton suffered from an inguinal hernia or gap in the abdominal muscle wall, which as it worsened would have produced a bulge near his groin.

There are things Creighton could have done to increase or decrease the risk, but the key point is that neither the hernia nor the strangulated intestine could not have been caused by a bad swing or any one thing that occurred in a particular baseball game or cricket match. It is possible that the pain that Creighton felt in the cricket match of October 9th or in the baseball game of October 14th was the existing hernia tearing or widening, but that in itself would not have been life-threatening. People with hernias can push protruding tissue back in place with no lasting bad effects. If they do not or cannot, however, a strangulated intestine may result. It is also possible that Creighton already had a strangulated intestine, and a gangrene infection had already set in, before he played cricket on October

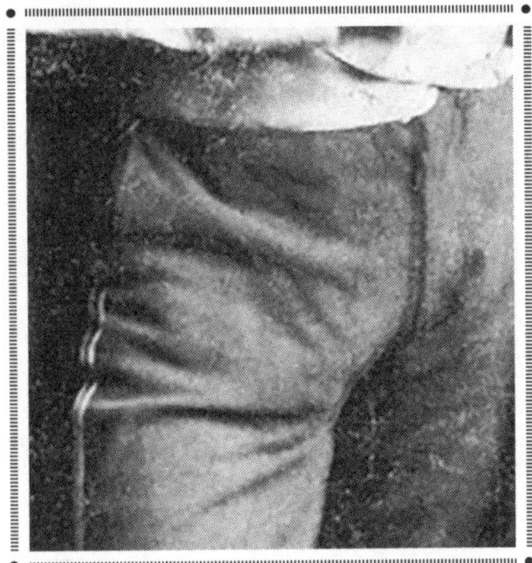

Inguinal hernias were well understood in Creighton's day; he would likely have been wearing a protective truss. This photograph of James Creighton seems to show a truss-like object underneath his uniform pants.

9th, 1862, and that what looked to others like a traumatic injury was actually worsening pain and discomfort from an existing infection.

Creighton's 1860 baseball season makes a much better suspect. Creighton carried his biggest workload that year. He pitched in twenty-one games, completing almost all of them. By a conservative estimate he threw about 160 innings. That does not sound like a tremendous amount, but Creighton's innings were not the same as those of modern pitchers — or of his contemporaries. Conventional pitchers like Mattie O'Brien, who ran up to the pitching line and did not throw nearly as hard as Creighton, put far less stress on their bodies than Creighton did, with his one-stride, uncoiling delivery. James Creighton was the original example of what we call today a "max effort" pitcher. In the terminology of 1860, he "put all his muscle in." Counting innings is also misleading. An average MLB pitcher today throws about fifteen pitches per inning, so a 160-inning season would mean about 2,400 pitches. In Creighton's day, pitchers averaged 30–45 pitches per inning. When James Creighton pitched 160 innings, he would have totaled 5,000 to 7,500 pitches — the equivalent in today's game of between 300 and 500 innings. No one in MLB has thrown 300 innings since the Orioles' Jim Palmer did it in 1977; for the last 500-inning pitcher we have to go back to 1892, the year before the pitching distance was lengthened to the current 60 feet, 6 inches. Unlike Palmer, however, Creighton was not pitching in a rotation, getting regular rest or receiving modern medical treatment. The Excelsiors did not play every day, but when they did, Creighton pitched virtually every inning. How much more he threw during the Excelsiors' weekly practice days is not known.

When we follow the 1860 season, game by game, through the game stories and the box scores, we can detect telltale signs that James Creighton was breaking down physically. The reason that pitchers threw so many pitches in the 1850s and 1860s was that there was no strike zone. If batters do not have to worry about being called out on strikes, they can wait as long as they want for their perfect pitch. This was happening more and more before Creighton. We do not have pitch counts for most games from that time, but in the first game of the Fashion Course series, Thomas Van Cott threw 208 pitches for New York; the Brooklyn pitchers combined for 339 pitches. The problem got worse after Creighton. If you do not have to, why would you swing at a pitch you cannot hit? Creighton threw so hard and was so unhittable that opposing hitters took what Henry Chadwick called "the waiting game" to an extreme. Unable to catch up with his fastball or handle his curve, they rested their bats on their shoulders, watched pitch after pitch go by, and waited for him to get tired. Their only chance of hitting the unhittable Creighton was if he lost velocity or made a mistake.

Creighton pitched every inning but one of the six games in nine days the Excelsiors played in their 1860 upstate tour. Against the Niagaras in Buffalo, Creighton threw 244 pitches. A manager who let a pitcher throw 144 pitches in a game today would be fired. In the second game of the championship series with the Atlantics, Creighton threw a surreal 280 pitches in seven innings. There were games in which Creighton threw over 80 pitches in an inning, which is close to a night's work for a modern starting pitcher. As consistently dominant as he was, however, he tended to tire in the late innings. In 1860 Creighton gave up only ten total runs in the first inning all season. He gave up nine in the second inning. In the seventh inning, however, he allowed 33 runs—39% of his season total. Creighton allowed 59% of his season run total in the seventh inning or later.

James Creighton also played cricket in 1860. He took up the sport that summer as a complete novice. He played in eight matches with different clubs or *ad hoc* elevens, mostly appearing as a bowler, the cricket equivalent of a pitcher in baseball. It is hard to evaluate how much this added to his workload, but in August of 1860 there was a stretch in which he was clearly overdoing it. On August 4th, Creighton pitched nine innings against the Putnams. Five days later was game two of the championship series versus the Atlantics, in which Creighton became too exhausted to continue pitching after the seventh inning. On August 19th, Creighton started against the Empire Club but had to stop pitching in the fourth because his arm was sore, reportedly from "having been practicing bowling recently." August 23rd was game three of the Atlantics series. The next day he bowled for the Long Island Cricket Club against Flatbush and the day after that, Creighton pitched nine innings against the Knickerbockers in Red Hook.

It might seem strange that James Creighton, a rising superstar in a rising American sport, would give aid and comfort to the enemy's national sport — not to mention risk his health — by playing both baseball and cricket at once. We know that important New York sports figures like Henry Chadwick and Henry Sharp encouraged him to play both sports. In New York, the cricket community was split between Englishmen and anglophiles who were content to keep cricket in an expatriate bubble; and those who tried to grow the sport by promoting it to native-born Americans; they hoped it would become America's national sport or at least co-exist with baseball as *a* national sport. Chadwick, who was born in the UK and who played cricket into late middle age, and Sharp, who was president of the New York Cricket Club, longtime rivals of New York City's preeminent cricket organization, the St. George Club, also belonged to baseball clubs. Both of these cricket clubs were made up almost exclusively of Englishmen. Chadwick was made an honorary member of the Stars; Sharp belonged to the Excelsiors. Henry Chadwick believed that cricket could succeed in America if it could be Americanized. That meant becoming less quirky and clannish, faster paced, and cleaner — meaning less compromised by gambling and professionalism. While baseball was ostensibly amateur, cricket allowed paid professionals, usually bowlers, to play side by side with true amateurs. It considered gambling good clean fun, and hiring a ringer to bowl in a big match was winked at as mere gamesmanship.

Chadwick wanted to use the star power of famous baseball players to sell cricket to the American public. In 1861 he helped found the American Cricket Club, which initially excluded anyone not born in the US. The club included baseball players from the Excelsiors, Atlantics, Stars and Putnams, among them Creighton, Leggett, Pearce, Dakin and Pearsall. Most members of the American Cricket Club were socially ambitious, well-to-do men, some of whom grew up playing the sport. They were in it because they enjoyed cricket and for its prestige. Others were from poorer backgrounds and made a living directly or indirectly from athletics. For them, cricket was an economic opportunity. James Creighton was in this category.

Henry Chadwick's dreams for American cricket were not realized. The American Cricket Club did produce several good American cricketers, but this contributed, ironically, to the club's demise. Until the 1820s, cricketers bowled underhand, like pitchers in early baseball. By the 1860s, however, bowling arm angles were moving up, reaching sidearm, and bowlers were pushing against the rule requiring delivering the ball with a straight arm and an unbent elbow. As a bowler, James Creighton dissented from both trends. He refitted his powerful pitching delivery to create a retro style of bowling that cricketers called "half-underarm shooters" that moved "like lightning." Creighton became an effective bowler in no time and the St. George Cricket Club noticed. Known as the "Dragonslayers," the St. George Club generally excluded American players, but winning was winning and money was money. The American Cricket Club changed their rules to allow members to play for more than one club at a time. The stated reason was "for the purpose of [members] obtaining a more thorough practical knowledge of the game," but the real purpose was to legitimize the St. Georges' poaching of James Creighton. Baseball did something similar by interpretating its own rule against paying players to define compensation as payment in cash, excluding payment in the form of jobs and real estate. This was convenient for the Excelsiors, because it allowed them to maintain that they were amateur, but that may have been the actual purpose. It is a measure of James Creighton's impact as an athlete that two different sports bent their rules for him.

By August of 1862 Creighton was playing for the Dragonslayers and the American Cricket Club was on the way out. In the March 7th, 1863, *Wilkes' Spirit of the Times,* Henry Sharp wrote that the late James Creighton, "had proved that he possessed the *materiel* likely to eventuate in his becoming one of the leading batsmen of the day," and gave highlights of Creighton's cricket career. As a batter, "on no occasion was he 'stumped' or got 'b.b.w.' [both are bad outcomes], which is what very few batsmen can say." But "his great forte was his bowling, very fast, underhand, with great 'work' [movement] from the off to the on [into a righthander's hands]. His great *coup-de-main* [surprise attack] in bowling was in 1860, against eleven Englishmen of the St. George, when he took five wickets in six balls [roughly equivalent to pitching a perfect game in baseball]."

There was a reason that James Creighton began to play more cricket (and less baseball) in 1861 and 1862) other than the fact that he was good at it and that it paid well—to give his body a break from baseball. Because cricket bowlers deliver the ball on the run, there is less twisting and less stress on the abdomen. Even in a full-length cricket match, bowlers bowl far fewer balls than Creighton pitched in a baseball game. Cricket limited the number of balls delivered to each batter. We have statistics for most of Creighton's twenty or so cricket matches that include the total number of balls that he bowled. They range generally from around 80 to 180 and average 120—in other words, about the same as the number of pitches thrown by a major league starter in nine innings today. James Creighton was both working harder and throwing two or three times as many pitches when he played baseball.

The Excelsiors themselves were aware of Creighton's inguinal hernia and what it meant. The club was full of medical doctors, including President Joseph Jones, club cofounders Van Brunt Wyckoff and Daniel Dodge—even first baseman and future traitor Aleck Pearsall, a friend and teammate of Creighton's who shared a dressing room with him. If you were diagnosed with an inguinal hernia today, your doctor would tell you to avoid strenuous exercise, particularly anything that involves extreme strain or violent twisting of the abdomen. They would have said the same thing in 1860. The Excelsiors, however, put Creighton on a demanding weight training program and sent him out to pitch almost every inning of every game they played that season. "Violent twisting of the abdomen" is a good shorthand description of

James Creighton's pitching delivery.

The Excelsiors could have moderated Creighton's workload, but instead they worked him like a rented mule. Baseball, not cricket, killed James Creighton. And baseball knew it. The Excelsior baseball club paid guilt money for Creighton's splendid grave monument, which is among the finest of the hundred thousand monuments in Green-Wood cemetery. Baseball's guilty conscience explains what was said, and not said, in the months and years after October 18th, 1862. When we feel guilt or shame, it is human nature to try to shift the blame for our actions to others or to avoid the subject. Consciousness of guilt explains the stupid dispute that broke out between cricket and baseball after Creighton died. Remember that the initial news reports said that Creighton suffered his fatal injury while batting in the October 14th game against the Unions. Excelsiors president Dr. Joseph Jones, Henry Chadwick and other pillars of the baseball establishment spoke out, trying to pin the blame on a different supposed injury that Creighton had suffered five days earlier in a cricket match between the St. George and the Willow Clubs. This was disingenuous and intended to muddy the waters. Henry Chadwick, Joseph Jones and the entire Excelsiors membership knew perfectly well that Creighton did not die from a traumatic injury that occurred on either occasion. They also knew that Creighton's deteriorating health was caused by overuse as a pitcher, not by hitting.

The Excelsiors needed James Creighton if they were to succeed in their mission to nationalize baseball; and they needed him if they were going to have any chance of taking the championship away from the Atlantics. He was absolutely indispensable. They knew that they were overworking him and risking his health — possibly even his life — but they did it anyway. In today's baseball, pitchers' bodies are routinely exploited to win games and championships. This is shrugged at as the cost of doing business, but it does not usually cost a life. James Creighton was both baseball's first pitching victim and the worst. This is why so little was said about James Creighton the person, even as his fame outlasted him. Respects were paid and

Creighton was revered as an abstraction, a martyred hero with a spotless character. Dozens of his teammates and opponents lived long lives, giving interviews, telling stories and writing memoirs about the glory days of the old Excelsiors, without saying much of anything about James Creighton as a human being. Instead of colorful anecdotes or interesting quotations, we have the tremendous impact he had on baseball and on America. The rest is silence.

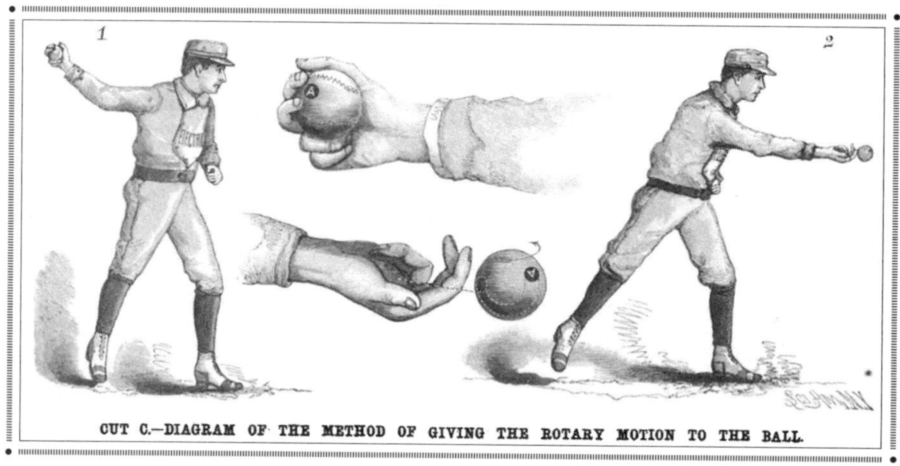

An illustration showing the illegal "throwing" delivery adopted by pitchers who could not master Creighton's legal curve. It was legalized in the 1870s and is still used today, although with an overhand delivery.

9 INSIDE THE BOX

THE GREATEST PLAYERS dominate the game. A rare few change the game.

The obvious example is Babe Ruth. Poster infant for the swing-for-the-fences, fans-on-their-feet Home Run Era, the Babe singlehandedly demonstrated that long fly balls score more runs than line drives. Ruth did not invent the home run, but he invented hitting a hell of a lot of them. When Ruth became a full-time hitter in 1920, the career major league home run record was 138. Ruth finished up with 714 home runs, a number that remains unmatched by anyone who wasn't Hank Aaron or who didn't have pharmaceutical assistance. Americans loved home run baseball, and they came out to see it in droves. When did the Home Run Era end? It didn't. Baseballs are still flying over fences, major-league turnstiles are still spinning, and today's fans cannot get enough of launch angles and exit velo.

James Creighton had a bigger impact on baseball than Babe Ruth. It is not even close. Ruth changed the way batters swung, but Creighton changed the deep structure of the game itself. His style of pitching was so unhittable that baseball literally had to invent the strike zone to deal with it. It is possible that without Creighton baseball might have evolved in a different direction. Think about that for a minute. We can conceive of a kind of baseball that does not rely on the home run. If you saw a game in the old Astrodome—to paraphrase Mark Twain—hell, you've seen it done. But it is a lot harder to picture baseball with no strike zone. The battle of hitter versus pitcher for control of the imaginary box hovering over home plate is more than the center of the action in modern baseball; it *is* the action. It is where games are won and lost, and it is at the heart of baseball's appeal to spectators. It is what we are watching on a TV screen, a smart phone or whatever we will be using to watch ballgames ten years from now.

Umpires did not call balls and strikes when Creighton played. Batters swung long, heavy bats and aimed for contact; they hardly ever struck out. They never walked. In no-strike-zone-baseball, the pitcher tossed the ball toward home plate and the batter swung if he felt like it. For decades, perhaps centuries, this worked. As long as anyone could remember, baseball had relied on a tacit understanding that the pitcher would put the ball where the batter could reach it, and the batter would swing at hittable pitches. This understanding was becoming strained under the rising competitive pressures of the late 1850s, but after being embarrassed by Creighton, batters broke their end of the bargain irrevocably and forever. They simply refused to swing, sometimes letting 40, 50 or 60 pitches go by. Something had to be done.

The strike zone was not born fully formed. It was the last domino to fall—the final result of rules changes that took place over two decades—but the first domino was James Creighton's pitching revolution. We can trace a direct line from Creighton to the creation of the strike zone. Because we view early baseball history through the imperfect lens of contemporary journalism, that line is sometimes blurry. Newspaper stories of the 1860s often give us the uncomfortable feeling that their authors did not entirely understand what they were looking at. We can usually rely on the information they provide, but the same cannot be said of their attempts at analysis.

Take, for example, the question of whether James Creighton was violating the pitching rules. We have it on the highest authority, expert contemporary eyewitnesses, that Creighton's pitching was legal. This was the opinion of both baseball's premier journalist (and future chairman of the rules committee) Henry Chadwick, and Pete O'Brien, the respected captain of the Atlantic Club of Brooklyn. Both of these men saw Creighton pitch with their own eyes. O'Brien faced him as a batter and umpired games that Creighton pitched. The problem is that ten years after Creighton died, both of these unimpeachable authorities started saying the exact opposite. Even worse, they did not explain why they had changed their minds or even admit that they had; they simply rewrote their own testimony, ignoring what they had said before. To this day, historians tend to follow their lead and tell us that James Creighton was cheating, ignoring all evidence to the contrary. Part of the reason for this lies in the nature of storytelling: cheating, crime and scandal are more interesting than prosaic truth. (This is a pattern that repeats itself in history. The Roman Emperor Tiberius was probably not a sexual pervert who threw people off the cliffs of Capri for fun, but that is more interesting to read about than his fiscal reforms.)

Remember Creighton's July 1859 debut as a pitcher for the Niagaras? Pete O'Brien was one of the veteran baseball men who was on the scene and who apparently saw nothing wrong with Creighton's pitching. O'Brien and his Atlantics faced Creighton in game one of the championship series on July 19th, 1860. There was a lot riding on this game. Again, no complaint was heard from the umpire or the Atlantics, who were dominated by Creighton, 23–4. Two weeks later, Creighton pitched for the Excelsiors against the Putnams. Pete O'Brien was the umpire. Henry Chadwick was there, too. By his own account, he went there for the express purpose of "[watching Creighton's] movements pretty closely, in order to ascertain whether he did pitch fairly or not." Chadwick concluded that Creighton's pitching was "unquestionably" legal. Chadwick added that he wondered why "such experienced batsmen as the Atlantics could ever be mastered by it." He also mentioned that umpire Pete O'Brien "seemed to be watching Creighton's pitching closely, and as he made no objections as to its fairness, we presume that it met with his entire approval." Compare this to what Henry Chadwick wrote when recalling game one of the 1860 championship series forty-five years later:

> Peter O'Brien went to the bat first, and Creighton retired him on strikes. The veteran was a sure hitter and Creighton's swift pitching bothered him. As he came in from the bat the veteran said, "Mr. Chadwick, that man throws underhanded; he could never get that speed from a square [legal] pitch."

In the 1860 version of this anecdote, it was clear to both Chadwick and O'Brien that Creighton was pitching legally. In 1902 he was clearly cheating by "throwing," i.e., illegally snapping his wrist.

It is not until around 1872 that a consensus emerged that James Creighton had been "throwing." Up to that point, Creighton's pitching was typically described as different, extremely fast, extremely accurate and with "considerable twist"—but not illegal. Someone could write a long (and boring) PhD thesis on what sportswriters of the 1860s and 1870s meant by the word "twist," but before the advent of the curveball—or the word "curveball"—*twist* was a very elastic word in the hands of sportswriters. It could be stretched to refer to any kind of pitch that was not perfectly straight, from a fastball with "life" to a true breaking pitch, and everything in between. Around 1872 and 1873, however, journalists started to call James Creighton a cheater. They did not back up their accusation with any facts; they simply asserted that Creighton was using a "disguised underhand throw," as if this had always been self-evident.

In the *New York Clipper* in 1872 Henry Chadwick wrote, with uncharacteristic snark:

> In the early days...before the advent of Creighton, the ball was generally delivered by a square pitch...but when Creighton came upon the scene and inaugurated the style of delivery which by courtesy has been called "swift pitching," the old style was not long in becoming defunct.

He added the following fishy anecdote.

> In 1858 during the visit of the English cricketers to this country, Creighton was one day bowling in a little practice game of cricket while John Lillywhite [an English cricketer who, ironically, was accused of bowling illegally] was looking on. Creighton at the time was noted as the great swift "pitcher" of the day and was bowling just as he pitched in baseball. While watching him Lillywhite quietly remarked, "why, that man is not bowling, he is throwing underhand"...It is the best

> disguised under-hand throwing I ever saw and might readily be mistaken for a fair delivery." [Only] two or three persons heard the comments of the noted cricketer, and as there was nothing ever said further about its legitimacy, Creighton's delivery was never questioned in the baseball fraternity...

Historians have made much mischief with this story, which is cited as evidence that Creighton was cheating by using a "disguised" wrist snap, in violation of the rules of both cricket and baseball. No disrespect meant to the great Henry Chadwick, but it does not add up. The English cricket tour took place in 1859, not in 1858. James Creighton was not "noted at the time as the great 'swift' pitcher" because had not yet started pitching in 1858. This conversation could not have happened in 1859, either, because Creighton did not start playing cricket until 1860, when Lillywhite was not in America. The biggest problem is that Creighton's bowling delivery in cricket was never "no-balled [ruled to be illegal]" or even questioned by anyone we know of, in any of the twenty-odd cricket matches he played in from 1860–1862. It sounds like Henry Chadwick made this story up, which could explain why he says that Lillywhite made his remark so "quietly" that hardly anyone heard him.

Henry Chadwick was right about one thing. James Creighton raised the velocity bar for all pitchers. "When Creighton introduced his well-disguised underhand throw," Chadwick wrote in 1873, "the old style of pitching went out of practice and speed became the great object in view" After July 1859, if a club wanted to compete at the highest level, it had to find someone who could pitch fast.

Why did Chadwick and others decide, long after the fact, that Creighton had been cheating? How did baseball get from fast pitching—legal and otherwise—to the strike zone? The answers to both questions lie in the period of time from Creighton's first pitch in 1859 to the year 1872. In 1872 the rules were relaxed to allow pitchers to "throw" openly, and to raise their arm angle above dead underhand. The story of baseball's first post-Creighton decade is the need for speed, the success and failure of the pitchers who tried to copy Creighton, and how the rules makers attempted to keep up.

Since the beginning of baseball time, a strike had been a pitch that the hitter swung at and missed. There were no *called* strikes or balls until 1858. That year a new rule was introduced. "Should a striker [batter] stand at the bat," it read, "without striking [swinging] at good balls repeatedly pitched to him...the umpire after warning him shall call one strike and if he persists...two and three strikes...." The 1858 rule is sometimes cited as evidence that pitchers were throwing hard before Creighton, but that is not it. The problem it was written to address was not batters playing the waiting game because they were overmatched; it was that pitches got past the catcher so frequently that when a batter reached first, the next man often adopted the sensible tactic of waiting for him to advance on a passed ball or wild pitch before putting a ball in play so he could drive him in with a single.

James Creighton was born in 1841. The first disruption he caused was to make slow and medium paced pitching obsolete. After 1859, pitchers like Tom Van Cott, Frank Pidgeon, William Bell, Tom Dakin and Joe Pinckney could no longer win at the top level. The second disruption came when the generation of pitchers a few years younger than him—born between 1843 and 1848—tried to copy him. Beside Excelsiors Brainard and Cummings, who had the advantage of studying under Creighton's catcher and pitching guru, Joe Leggett, the most successful successors to Creighton were Dick McBride, Tom Pratt and Joseph Sprague. Born near Boston, Pratt pitched in three cities between 1863 and 1871: Philadelphia, Brooklyn and Boston. In 1863 he was "universally acknowledged as the best [pitcher] in [Philadelphia]." In 1869 Chadwick called Pratt "without a doubt, the greatest [pitcher] after James Creighton." He is described as having excellent control, but he could also be effectively wild when he needed to intimidate batters. When Pratt moved to Brooklyn for business reasons, he pitched for the Atlantics; his place in Philadelphia was taken by McBride. Writing in the *New York Clipper* in 1866, Henry Chadwick described McBride's pitching as "perfectly fair" and "characterized by a thoroughly straight arm, and a perpendicular [dead underhand] swing in delivery." In other words, both Pratt and McBride pitched legally, very fast and with good control. In 1874, the *Clipper* said that "McBride was the first man to get hold of Creighton's style, though Pratt was quite effective." We only have to look at the won-lost records of the top clubs to see the impact of the Creighton imitators. The best clubs of 1863 were the Eckfords (with Sprague), the Atlantics (with Pratt) and the Athletics (with McBride).

In 1862 Joe Sprague accomplished what Creighton came so excruciatingly close to doing in 1860—dethroning the Atlantics. Sprague and the Eckfords then defended their championship in 1863. Sprague had been unavailable to pitch in the first two games of the 1862 Atlantics series because he was away at the war with the Thirteenth New York State Militia. He was mustered out six days before the deciding game three in late September. A total of seventy-eight runs had been scored in games one and two, but with Sprague—even a Sprague with three months' worth of rust—it was a different ballgame. The Eckfords took the deciding game by the dazzling score of 8–3. "As for the *how* of their doing it," wrote *Wilkes' Spirit of the Times*, "we must refer all of our readers to pitcher Sprague."

Eyewitness descriptions of Joe Sprague's pitching could pass for descriptions of Creighton. Years later, teammates even swore that Sprague threw Creighton's underhand, rising curveball. Like Creighton, Sprague played cricket, although certainly not because he needed the money. Descended from two socially prominent Brooklyn families and the grandson of a mayor, Sprague was a wealthy eccentric (with an interesting love life) who had no interest in sports as a career. He quit pitching after 1863 at twenty years old, made a comeback in 1869 and then returned to cricket; he played baseball again as an amateur in the 1870s. An 1879 story about a cricket match between Brooklyn players and a visiting All-England cricket eleven led by Richard Daft, one of the top batsmen of the day, contains an intriguing description of the 36-year-old Sprague's "fast, underhand" bowling style, which sounds like Creighton's bowling. "Captain Daft," it was reported, "was clean bowled by Sprague, an old baseball player." To be clean bowled is like striking out in baseball, but it is rarer in cricket and a much greater disaster for a batsman.

The changing of the guard was swift. Before the grass had time to grow over James Creighton's grave, every top club that had not already found a fast pitcher was desperately searching for one. Bernie Hannegan, of course, pitched against Creighton for the Unions of Morrisania in 1862. In 1863 the Mutuals used Billy McKeever; the Atlantics had Pratt; the Athletics had McBride and the Excelsiors replaced Creighton with Asa Brainard. By 1865, the Active Club had Charley Walker, the Eckfords had George Zettlein; and the Nationals had Billy Williams. None of them was the full Creighton; in 1865 Henry Chadwick wrote that "[Creighton's] pitching was of the swiftest possible order. It has never been approached since his death," but all of them had velocity. Baseball's problem was that there were not enough effective Creighton imitators to go around. The first post-Creighton pitching generation falls into two categories. There were the McBrides, Pratts and Brainards who, like Creighton, had speed, movement and command. The rest were fast and wild. Some were very wild. The most outrageous member of the wild bunch was Bernie Hannegan.

Years later, when Henry Chadwick got it into his head that James Creighton and his more successful successors had been using an illegal, "well-disguised underhand throw," Chadwick bizarrely maintained that Hannegan's problem was that he was *not* cheating. "We well remember 'Creighton in his palmiest days,'" wrote Chadwick in 1874, "and the way he used to scare batsmen with his pace was noteworthy. But the most effective part of his pitching—underhand throwing, we mean—was his thorough command of the ball. His success tempted dozens of players to strive to equal him in pace and accuracy of aim. The former they could succeed in, but in the latter they failed, and why? We will tell you...Hannegan went in strong for speed and tried in vain to succeed in command of the ball; but instead of the underhand throw delivery, he sent the ball in by a square [legal] pitch, and he did so with all the speed at his command, the result was that not one ball in six went near enough the bat to be hit. A wilder pitcher never handled the ball... the games in which Hannegan pitched became noted for their tedious length...frequently occupying four hours."

Reporting on an October 1862, 13–10 victory by the Eckfords over the Unions, Chadwick sounds like a man who could not take anymore.

> The cry against [Hannegan's pitching style] is almost universal. Strictly speaking it is a pitch, but conscientiously it is not. Nothing can be gained by it. In the end it will injure ball playing more than is thought. It is not only bothersome to the striker, who is kept waiting for a ball, but delays the game, and deadens all the interest.... This new style of pitching is daily gaining ground, and the only reason...is that every player, if he can throw a ball, is capable of mastering it....What a vast difference there is between Hannigan's pitching and that of Creighton, and Sprague.... In the match on Tuesday, in the third inning, Hannigan had pitched 60 balls, 26 of which were over the striker's head....

A year later, baseball had still not found an answer. This is from a game story from 1863.

> About the most tedious, dull and in fact, stupid game of ball we have witnessed this season, was that played yesterday...the miserable pitching on both sides, but especially of that of Hannegan ...[made] it one of the dullest affairs ever seen on a ball ground. Three hours were occupied in playing five innings, two being taken up in getting through the first three innings, this waste of time arising from the wild pitching of [Hannegan], who surpassed himself in his peculiar style of delivering the ball....

There was one other problem. With no incentive to throw strikes, pitchers started throwing the ball at hitters to intimidate them. In the 1860s the hit-by-pitch rule did not exist. Imagine putting Pedro Martinez on the mound with no called balls and no penalty for hitting the batter—it would be *criminal.* As one writer deadpanned, "Both pitchers interpreted the rule of the game, requiring them to pitch 'for the striker' to mean 'at the striker.'"

In 1864 baseball acted. Called balls were introduced. Baseball had been pushing umpires to call more strikes for years with mixed success, but under the new rule, umpires were now required to call balls — again, only after repeated bad pitches and a verbal warning. Four called balls and the batter would reach first base. (In practice, this meant many more than four, because umpires waited before issuing warnings and even then, they did not call a ball on every bad pitch.) The brains behind the famous "Sixth Rule," who very likely saved baseball as entertainment, were Dr. Jones of the Excelsiors and Dr. William Bell. We get a glimpse of how visionary they were in an experiment they conducted early in the 1864 season. The Empires were playing the Actives at the Elysian Fields in Hoboken. As Henry Chadwick wrote, "a novel definition of the sixth rule of the game by Mr. McMahon of the Mutual Club, who acted as umpire in the match, changed the contest... into an experimental game, and one of the quickest... ever played." Channeling current MLB Commissioner Rob Manfred, McMahon told both teams that he intended to pick up the pace by calling every single pitch a ball or a strike, no warnings issued. "This exceedingly strict, and, in fact, erroneous interpretation of the rule, of course created considerable astonishment...." After some complaining, the experiment went forward and "ultimately... considerable fun [was] had by the majority." "Fun" was not a word that Chadwick tossed around casually. With Dr. Bell pitching, the Empires won, 29–16, and treated the crowd to a preview of baseball's future. Even with forty-five runs crossing the plate, the game was completed in one hour and thirty-five minutes — roughly the average duration of a major league game in the 1910s.

Called balls and strikes raised the degree of difficulty for pitchers again. After Creighton, pitchers had to have velocity in order to compete, but now they had to have Creighton-like command as well. With the rules still requiring a straight-arm, dead underhand delivery, with no "throwing," or wrist snap, allowed, most of them simply could not do it. Pitchers did what ballplayers have always done when they cannot succeed with luck, talent and hard work. They cheated.

If they could get away with it, "throwing"—snapping their wrist—and "jerking"—straightening a bent elbow during delivery—meant that they could pitch with better control and more speed, even if they were not in James Creighton's class as athletes. They discovered that it is much easier to throw a curveball this way than the way Creighton did it. It took a few seasons of controversy and pushing against the rulebook; umpires frequently pushed back, ruling that pitchers were throwing illegally. But as the umpires began to tolerate subtle forms of illegal throwing, more pitchers found that they could throw harder with better control, and almost all of them mastered the curveball. The curve is more effective from a higher arm angle, which led to more bending of the rule requiring a dead-underhand arm motion. In 1872, the baseball rules committee gave up. It legalized "throwing" and allowed pitchers to raise their arm angle to just below sidearm.

For baseball, the changes of 1872 were progress. For baseball history, not so much.

Remember that when James Creighton was in his prime, no sportswriters, not even Henry Chadwick, were sure exactly what he was doing with the baseball to make it travel so fast and with such precise location and movement. They still were not sure after McBride, Pratt and Sprague achieved a reasonable facsimile of Creighton's style of pitching. But after watching the pitchers of the late 1860s and the early 1870s cheat their way to something like what they remembered Creighton doing, they jumped to the wrong conclusion—Creighton must have been cheating, too, but we could not tell because he was so good at it!

"It is now well known," wrote the *New York Times* in 1872, "that from the time of the reign of Creighton up to the present day, the style of a swift delivery of the ball to the bat has been by an underhand throw, and not by a square pitch, it being simply impossible for any man to send a ball in by a square, straight-arm pitch with [that kind of] speed...." The same paper, two years later: "The delivery that admits at once of great speed and complete command of the ball is the low underhand throw, made with the arm swinging nearly perpendicularly to the side of the body [almost sidearm]. This style of 'pitching'—if we may call it so—was first introduced by Creighton, who united a rapid pace with the most thorough command of the ball." This is just not true. Creighton did not raise his arm angle an inch; he pitched dead underhand, as the rules required.

One anonymous reporter came closest to identifying the true dynamic at work here. "Those pitchers," he wrote, "who failed in achieving the success attained by the lamented Creighton offset their want of skill by trying to intimidate the batsmen." James Creighton did not break the baseball pitching rules. He transcended them, defeating their intent without doing anything illegal. One way we know this is that some of his imitators successfully adopted his style of pitching, without breaking the rules and without sacrificing command for speed. The majority of post-Creighton pitchers, however, were not capable of pitching the way Creighton did. They were fast but they were so wild that they almost ruined the game.

The irony is that both kinds of pitchers—Creighton and his disciples; and Hannegan and the wild bunch—helped push baseball toward modern pitching and the strike zone. By the end of the 1880s, pitchers threw fastballs and curveballs, and umpires called every pitch a ball or a strike according to whether it passed through the imaginary box prescribed by the rulebook. The James Creighton pitching revolution was victorious; the old order was gone. From that time on, the game they were playing was modern baseball.

10 WHAT HAPPENED TO...

THE CREIGHTONS

James Creighton died unmarried and childless. He left behind an elderly father; a brother, John; and a sister, Mary Ann. Both of Creighton's siblings had descendants whose stories do not belong in this book. But baseball makes a surprise return appearance in Mary Ann Creighton's family line.

Next to James Creighton's impressive monument in Green-Wood cemetery is a small stone decorated with an American flag. The military veteran buried beneath it is John Creighton. As a biographical subject John Creighton is the mirror opposite of his younger brother James. James Creighton's personality is a blank; we know him by his works. John Creighton is eminently knowable. He began as a minor player in the raucous Bowery Boy and Tammany Hall Democratic politics of the 1850s. He later commanded citizen militias, worked for politicians from Isaiah Rynders to Fernando Wood, ran for Congress and lost (which was hard to do for a New York City Democrat), accompanied William Walker on his doomed errand in Nicaragua, served in the Civil War, and became a lawyer. We can read his bombastic speeches. If you search his name in a database of digitized nineteenth-century American newspapers, you will turn up far more information than if you searched his brother's name. John Creighton's life was full of color, but it had a *Zelig*-like quality. He often appears on the scene of a wide range of historical events, but unlike his younger brother, he is justly forgotten.

John Creighton rode a roller-coaster of success and failure. He showed flashes of brilliance and physical courage, but he was reckless and erratic. During William Walker's freelance invasion of Nicaragua in the mid 1850s, Creighton's quick thinking helped to save Walker's rag-tag army from disaster in the Battle of Santa Rosa. He then put a gun to the head of a Hungarian mercenary who had abandoned his post and threatened to pull the trigger. When the defeated Walker was executed, John Creighton was back in New York, having quit in disgust at Walker's cruelty and incompetence. Creighton was an alcoholic, but he was active in the Temperance movement and lectured on the evils of alcohol.

Officers of the 13th NY State Militia, among them commanding officer John B. Woodward (seated at left) and James Creighton's catcher and mentor Major Joseph Leggett (seated at right). Both Woodward and Leggett belonged to the Excelsior baseball club.

During the Civil War, volunteer regiments were raised by men with wide social and political connections; those who enlisted would then choose their own officers. Weeks after Fort Sumter, John Creighton broke with his pro-neutrality Tammany Hall bosses and answered Lincoln's call for volunteers to fight for the Union. He recruited hundreds of men for the Sixth New York Regiment and was elected lieutenant colonel. In October of 1861 he distinguished himself at an obscure Civil War battle in Florida that, weirdly enough, is also called the Battle of Santa Rosa. But then Creighton, for the umpteenth time, fell off the wagon. He was court-martialed for getting drunk and firing a rifle at a superior officer; he testified at trial that his only regret was that he had missed. His drinking and hotheadedness always got him in trouble, but his intelligence and knowledge of the law sometimes got him out. He challenged the court-martial on procedural grounds, negotiated an honorable discharge and went home to Brooklyn. There he moved from one occupation and scheme to another; he passed the bar but also worked as an auctioneer and a railroad superintendent. Another lifelong pattern was borrowing money from his father, James Creighton, Sr., investing it and losing it. When James Creighton, Sr. died in 1876, he left John's widow Sarah and her children nothing. Mary Ann Creighton inherited both Henry Street houses that her brother James's athletic talent had paid for. Sarah Creighton contested the will. There was a hearing at which a friend of James Creighton, Sr. explained that the elder Creighton had cut off his son John's family because he had "liberally provided" for them while John was alive.

In 1858 John Creighton married the daughter of a Brooklyn cabinet maker he had met at Temperance meetings, and had four sons who reached adolescence: James, William, Pearsall and Mortimer. The marriage had its ups and downs; Creighton lived with his wife's family until they could afford a place of their own. In 1870, according to the US Census, John Creighton was living with his father on Henry Street, along with his sons James and William. He was separated from his wife, who was living elsewhere with the two other boys. In 1873, John Creighton was in Topeka, Kansas, pursuing one of his hopeless business ventures. When it did not go well, he crawled into a bottle and stayed there for two weeks. On May 9, he shot himself fatally in his hotel room. One of his sons—either James, who was twelve, or William, nine—was there when it happened. In 1873 the Lawrence, Kansas *Daily Journal* identified John Creighton as "a brother of the celebrated baseball player of the same name." This is the first and only known time that the two Creighton brothers, both public figures, were linked in print. It tells us about John Creighton's post-Civil War reputation that Henry Chadwick and his fellow baseball writers would steer well clear of the topic of James Creighton's older brother.

Mary Ann Creighton had helped raise James, Jr. after their mother died in 1849. Her reward was to stay home and take care of her father, who never worked after moving to Brooklyn in 1857. In his eighties, James, Sr. suffered a stroke that left him partially paralyzed. In February of 1871, when she was 36, Mary Ann Creighton married a 38-year-old stockbroker named Charles Parkes. (He may be the "Parks" who played for the Charter Oak baseball club in the late 1850s.) But in October of 1872 he dropped dead of a heart attack, leaving the eight-months pregnant Mary Ann a widow. For the next four years, Mary Ann lived at 309 Henry and cared for her invalid father, who lived next door at 307 Henry, and raised her son, James Creighton Parkes. This is the same James Creighton Parkes, also a stockbroker, who in 1937 wrote a letter to the editor of the Brooklyn *Daily Eagle*, protesting the Hall of Fame's decision to honor Arthur Cummings, not his uncle, as the inventor of the curveball.

In the 1890s James Creighton Parkes and his mother sold the Henry Street houses, moved to the Upper East Side of Manhattan and then to suburban New Jersey. Parkes had a son named James S. Parkes, who in 1935 had a son that he named James Creighton Parkes after the child's grandfather. In 1957 the second James C. Parkes graduated from Dartmouth and in 1961 from Harvard Medical School. Parkes played Ivy League football and was a good amateur athlete. He skied, ran and played football, tennis and golf—but apparently not the sport that killed his great-great-uncle. Like Joe Leggett, he believed in weight training in sports at a time when it went against the conventional wisdom. Dr. Parkes was the team physician of the New York Mets for 18 years, served as president of the MLB Physicians Association, and famously helped the Knicks' Willis Reed get through the 1970 NBA finals with a leg injury. Parkes died in 1999, but that is not the end of the family's contributions to baseball. Dr. Parkes' daughter, Jacqueline Parkes, was MLB's Chief of Marketing from 2008 until 2016.

AMATEUR BASEBALL

IN HIS 1867 BOOK, *The Temper of Our Time*, Eric Hoffer wrote the immortal and usually misquoted sentence: "What starts out here as a mass movement ends up as a racket, a cult, or a corporation." Baseball the sport began as a reform movement. It shrewdly marketed itself to the Protestant middle classes, who disapproved of violence and gambling, as a clean alternative to the sleaziness of horseracing and boxing. Both to keep out corruption and to be seen as respectable, organized baseball originally felt that it had to be amateur. Has baseball today turned into a "racket, a cult, or a corporation?" Well, it is not a cult—unless you count youth travel teams.

Baseball succeeded wildly as a participant sport, but when baseball started to become entertainment, the door opened, and professionalism walked in. Less than a decade after the death of James Creighton, amateurs would no longer contend for national championships. Baseball's first governing body, the amateur New York City–based NABBP, effectively gave up its control over the sport in 1869, when it legalized clubs paying players, something that most of the top clubs were already doing in the shadows. This was followed by the epic run of the Cincinnati Red Stockings, a team made up entirely of talented—and paid—young mercenaries brought in (with one exception) from New York City, Brooklyn and elsewhere. Behind the Creighton-esque pitching of Asa Brainard, formerly the second-best pitcher on the 1860–1862 Excelsiors, the Red Stockings crisscrossed the country and went undefeated in eighty-four games from late 1868 to June of 1870. Everyone agrees that the Red Stockings set the stage for the National Association, the first professional baseball league, in 1871. This league was replaced by the present National League in 1876. The advent of professional baseball, however, did nothing to erase amateur baseball's success in achieving its main goals: becoming our first national sport and getting ordinary Americans interested in physical fitness. The amateur baseball movement deserves most of the credit for the fact that modern Americans, unlike their notoriously sedentary ancestors, run, work out and play competitive sports from childhood to old age.

The short answer to the question of what happened to amateur baseball is not a lot. It is alive and thriving. Virtually all 32,000 US high schools field baseball teams; three hundred D1 college teams play the game at a high level. Softball is a baseball world unto itself, with all of its sub-types played by a total of 10 million Americans last year. Outlawing professionalism had a purpose in the mid-nineteenth century, but that purpose was served. Would today's Major League Baseball be better if its players were unpaid, or paid under the table—or paid with favors, no-show jobs and real estate? It is hard to see how.

HENRY CHADWICK

Henry Chadwick lost much of his baseball insider status when the New York–based amateur NABBP self-destructed. He lost the rest of it when the New York–based professional National Association was replaced by the Midwest-centric National League in 1876. But Chadwick had already contributed much to baseball by promoting the game relentlessly, guiding the development of its rules, and inventing or adapting most of baseball's basic statistics, as well as coming up with the box score. Chadwick was the most important early baseball writer. He invented baseball's scoring system and most of its basic statistics. He had a long second act in the Professional Era as a journalist and editor of the *Spalding Guide* series, MLB's official annual for many decades. In 1908 Chadwick went to the Opening Day game between the Brooklyn Dodgers and the New York Giants, caught a cold and died. He was buried in Brooklyn's Green-Wood cemetery under a gorgeous, baseball-themed monument that is rivaled only by the nearby grave of James Creighton. Visitors leave baseballs here as well. An inscription on Chadwick's grave reads: "Father of Baseball."

Henry Chadwick's grave in Brooklyn's Green-Wood Cemetery, decorated with bronze baseball equipment. As with James Creighton's nearby monument, contemporary visitors leave behind baseballs as a gesture of respect.

Whether or not he or anyone was truly baseball's father, Chadwick did indirectly father baseball's phony baloney origin story, the so-called Abner Doubleday myth. In the early 1900s, Chadwick began to irritate his employer, sporting goods magnate and owner of the Chicago Cubs Albert Spalding, by publicly theorizing that the American national pastime of baseball had come from an English children's game called rounders. American Nativism had seen better days, but it was far from extinct in 1907. Spalding took Chadwick's theory as an insult to our national pride. He appointed a commission that pretended to investigate the origins of baseball. The commission members understood the assignment; it did not matter who invented baseball or where, as long as it was invented on American soil by a native-born American. They concluded, based on evidence that is hard to read out loud without laughing, that baseball had been invented by Doubleday in 1839 in Cooperstown, New York *and had no foreign origins*. This is the reason why today the National Baseball Hall of Fame is in Cooperstown, and not in Brooklyn, lower Manhattan or Hoboken, New Jersey.

THE EXCELSIORS

THE ATLANTICS AND ECKFORDS turned pro, but the Excelsiors were not interested. When baseball's governing body, the NABBP, created a new classification for openly professional clubs for the 1869 season, the Excelsiors said no thanks. Dead in the water after James Creighton's death and the loss of Joe Leggett and Asa Brainard, the club had a brief competitive renaissance in the post–Civil War years, thanks to talented local youngsters like Arthur Cummings, Herbert Jewell, and the Chauncey brothers. But they faded again in the 1870s. In 1878 they dropped baseball from their name and became one of New York's most exclusive social clubs — so exclusive, it was said, that no one in New York society was so elevated that he could feel slighted not to be admitted to the Excelsior Club. Two things finished off the Excelsiors. One was the Great Depression. The other was the demise of the community that the club belonged to. In the age of the automobile, the Brooklyn Bridge and mass transit, wealthy suburbanites who commuted to Wall Street moved to Long Island, Connecticut and New Jersey. Brooklyn became grubbier and more proletarian. When the club closed, its trophy baseballs, records and other possessions were distributed among the 12 remaining members. Where they are now is anyone's guess.

The Excelsiors' legacy includes their last clubhouse, a lovely Neo-Georgian rowhouse acquired by the club in the 1870s and sold to an Italian American social services agency in 1932. It still stands at the corner of Clinton and Livingstone Streets in Brooklyn Heights. A commemorative plaque was attached to it in 1974 that reads:

> This house was the former home of the Brooklyn Excelsiors, baseball champions of the United States in 1860. Constructed in 1851, the building was once the Jolly Young Bachelors clubhouse. The Bachelors evolved into the Excelsiors baseball team. One of its pitchers, James Creighton, 307 Henry Street, Brooklyn, is said to have tossed the first curve ball. During the Civil War, the Excelsiors introduced the game to soldiers from various states. Because of its popularity, similar teams were established in other cities. Thus, baseball, as a national sport, can be considered as having its origins in Brooklyn.

As historical plaques go, the accuracy of this one is about average. The Jolly Young Bachelors did not use this building. The Excelsiors did not move in until years after they ceased to be primarily a baseball organization; there was more whist and Wall Street gossip discussed within its walls than baseball. Of course, calling the Excelsiors champions of baseball in 1860 is dubious. The rest of it is defensible. Another physical remnant of the Excelsiors is their playing grounds, which were located near what is now Field #9 in Red Hook Park. You can go there today and watch high school kids play, unaware that they are playing where James Creighton pitched and where the world championship of baseball was once contested.

George Chauncey was born to a wealthy Brooklyn Heights family whose money came from real estate development. He and his brother Dan played for the Excelsiors in the late 1860s. A "never failing booster of Brooklyn," Chauncey was one of the few rich Brooklyn Heights boys who stayed when the neighborhood started to lose its cachet. Chauncey was president of the Excelsior social club in the 1880s. In 1890 he bankrolled the Brooklyn entry in the Players League, a third baseball major league that lasted one year. In 1891 he bought into the National League Brooklyn Bridegrooms. There he was impressed by a front office employee and decided to give the man stock in the club to keep him with the organization. The Bridegrooms became the Dodgers, and the front office employee was Charles Ebbets, who built Ebbets Field and owned and ran the club from 1898 to 1925.

THE ECKFORDS

THE ECKFORD BASEBALL CLUB was founded by men from three worlds: shipwrights and men who worked in related industries; fish dealers from the Fulton Market; and lovers of French cuisine. In the 1840s and 1850s shipwrights, ropemakers, dock builders and iron molders crossed the East River from Corlear's Hook in Manhattan to Greenpoint and Williamsburg, following the shipyards that employed them. What brought the three kinds of original Eckfords together was the Manor House, which was a short walk from the East River shoreline where the shipyards were located. It was also convenient to lower Manhattan by horsedrawn streetcar lines that linked to East River point-to-point ferries. Originally a farmhouse, the Manor House became a tavern and then a weekend resort that catered to hunters, fishermen, cricketers and baseball players. The Manor House was managed by French-speaking Belgians and featured excellent French food, which was rare in New York at that time; this explains the Frenchness of some of the first Eckfords. One important early Eckford, Pierre Tostevin, was born on the island of Jersey, which has spent the past 950 years or so in a cultural and political limbo, ruled by Britain but culturally largely French into the twentieth century. (In some censuses, Tostevin identifies his birthplace as France, in others as England.) He grew up playing cricket, which explains how a Frenchman became a first-rate baseball player. The Eckfords played their games in an open space in Wyckoff's Woods, a few hundred yards from the Manor House, that today is roughly bound by Herbert Street, North Henry Street, Richardson Street and Kingsland Avenue. The club moved to the Union Grounds in nearby Williamsburg in 1862.

The lost trophy case of the great Atlantic club of Brooklyn. A similar trophy case kept by the Eckfords of Greenpoint survives today in the National Baseball Hall of Fame Museum in Cooperstown.

Brooklyn's shipbuilding industry slumped after the Civil War, but other industries took its place. The Eastern District had a vibrant baseball scene and produced the playing talent that helped the Eckfords win two championships and, ultimately, supplied baseball clubs all over the country. Future Philadelphia Athletics slugger and cofounder of the National League Phillies Al Reach grew up around the corner from the Manor House and the Eckfords' playing grounds. Greenpoint and Williamsburg soon filled up with factories and the tenements that housed their immigrant workers. In the 1870s Greenpoint was well on its way to becoming the most Irish neighborhood in Brooklyn. St. Cecilia's Church was built on a piece of the Eckfords' old playing grounds; a Catholic school, convent and maternity hospitality took the rest.

In 1865 the Eckfords split into two clubs; one was a purely baseball organization, and the other a social and political club. The baseball Eckfords failed to navigate the transition to professional baseball, folding after one unsuccessful season in the National Association in 1872. The social club outlived it by ninety years. The Eckford Club disbanded in the mid-1960s, about the time that the last local Irish Americans moved to the suburbs. Unlike almost every other Amateur Era baseball club, the Eckfords closed up shop in a responsible and orderly way, donating all of their records, memorabilia and their case of trophy baseballs dating back to 1856 to the National Baseball Hall of Fame.

THE ATLANTICS

THE ECKFORDS AND THE EXCELSIORS passed out of existence because the communities that created and nurtured them disappeared. The Atlantics, however, came to represent a community that has never passed out of existence, the city of Brooklyn itself. Brooklyn refused to accept losing the Atlantics. The emotional connection between club and city was too strong. The club died, but the idea of the Atlantics did not.

The changing economics of baseball was part of the problem. In the late Amateur Era and the early Professional Era, baseball clubs who paid their players did so in one of three ways: with a salary, with a share of the gate receipts, and with no-show or sinecure positions, usually government jobs. This gave the Atlantics an advantage because of their access to political patronage jobs via the Brooklyn Democratic party and the Hugh McLaughlin machine. This ceased to be workable soon after the advent of national professional leagues, which raised overhead costs. It was replaced by a corporate model in which clubs sold stock to raise capital, separated management from labor and put players under contract.

The Atlantics' last hurrah was their miraculous, undefeated streak-breaking, extra-inning upset of the Cincinnati Red Stockings in June of 1870. The following season, the Atlantics declined to join the National Association and lost most of their veteran stars to professional clubs. In most baseball history books, this is where the story of the Atlantics ends. Individual Atlantics players continued their careers. There were clubs called Atlantic, but strictly speaking, they were distinct entities from the club that had dominated Amateur Era baseball.

If we take a wider view, however, the period from 1870–1884 tells a different story, the story of Brooklyn's determination to recover its place in the baseball world by reviving or replacing its beloved home team. In 1871, Brooklyn fans went to the Union Grounds in Williamsburg to root for the so-called New York Mutuals. The Mutuals might as well have played under the name Atlantics. They played all their home games in Brooklyn; they were managed by long-time Atlantic Bob Ferguson; and the Mutuals' lineup had Joe Start, Dickey Pearce and Charlie Smith—the core of the late Atlantics dynasty of the Amateur Era. In 1872, a different club calling itself the Atlantics joined the National Association. It was organized by ex-Atlantic star Jack Chapman, managed by Bob Ferguson, who also played third base, and had ex-Atlantics Jack Burdock and Jack Remsen. "Let Brooklyn have one prominent nine in the professional arena in 1872," wrote the Brooklyn *Daily Eagle*, "even if we have to furnish all the professional clubs in the country with their strongest players." This was not an exaggeration. The city of Brooklyn supplied twenty-three percent of the players in the first season of the National League and an even higher percentage in the National Association. The new, pro editions of the Atlantics, however, did not cover themselves with glory, finishing sixth in 1872, 1873 and 1874. They finished twelfth in 1875, the final season for both the name *Atlantics* and the National Association itself.

Eighteen-seventy-six was the first season of the National League, the same National League that is around today. A Brooklyn entry that would have brought back several old Atlantics players was talked about and fell through, but the 1876 National League Hartford, Connecticut Dark Blues were a kind of Brooklyn away from home. The club was managed by Bob Ferguson and had ex-Atlantics Burdock, Remsen, John Cassidy and Tommy Bond. Hartford resident Samuel Clemens rooted for this club, but Brooklyn fans followed them as well. There were more of them. The following year, Hartford added popular ex-Atlantics slugger Joe Start and moved all of their home games to Brooklyn to sell more tickets. Hartford dropped out of the league in 1878. For the next five years, Brooklyn baseball men planned and plotted to bring professional baseball back to Brooklyn, but the city remained on the outside looking in until 1883, when Charles Byrne formed a Brooklyn club that played in the Interstate Association, a minor league. Its home was Washington Park at the foot of Park Slope in Brooklyn, where Brooklyn's first baseball club, the Excelsiors, had played their first games in 1855. One year later Byrne's club entered the American Association, a major league; in

1890 it switched to the National League, where it would become known as the Brooklyn Dodgers.

Baseball abandoned Brooklyn once more in 1958, but the idea that Brooklyn deserves major league representation refuses to die. The Mets were a consolation prize of sorts; they gave Brooklynites a National League rooting interest, if not a home team. Today, Brooklyn has no major league baseball club, but it has the NBA Nets, making Brooklyn the only community that is not a city, state or region to be represented by a major league franchise in any of the four principal pro sports.

JOSEPH LEGGETT

EVER SINCE 1877, when James Creighton's catcher Joe Leggett got caught with his hand in the till at the Brooklyn Police Department, changed his name and went on the lam, his whereabouts have been a complete mystery. The old Excelsiors took care of each other, during and after their playing days, and it seems that some of them stayed in touch with Leggett. Henry Chadwick made it clear that he knew more than he could reveal in print, but in the 150 years since Leggett's disappearance both the public and baseball historians have been in the dark about where Leggett went, what he did and even when, where and how he died.

Over the past twenty years, I have spent many hours trying to find out what happened to Joe Leggett. It often seemed like mission impossible. Where do you begin to look for information about a man who was trying not to be found—and who died more than a century ago? How do you search records, newspapers and databases for a name you do not know? My starting point was a family genealogical record that gives a date of death, July 25, 1894, and a rumor that he died, perhaps in jail, in a place called Dickinson, which is fifteen miles from Galveston in southeast Texas. The only encouraging detail is the specificity of the date. I checked death and legal records in that part of Texas, hoping that I might find someone about Leggett's age who died on or around that date. Another hope was that Leggett might have used an alias that meant something to him—like, say, his mother's maiden name or the name of a place where he had lived. But I had no luck. There is a Dickinson town cemetery, but it has no headstone for someone who could be Leggett. Of course, that may mean that his grave was never marked, which would not have been unusual in that time. A bigger problem is that in 1900, the worst hurricane in American history killed at least eight thousand people in Galveston alone and flattened the surrounding area. If Joe Leggett had a wooden grave marker, a death record, or a court or jail record anywhere near Galveston, it would have been washed away. I checked state records, but most of them are unavailable or do not go back that far. I looked through local newspapers for a death notice of a man near Leggett's age. Galveston County had a lively baseball scene in the 1890s; I checked sports stories, records and memoirs on the off chance that someone who might be Leggett got involved in baseball somehow. None of these searches turned up anything.

Then, late one night about three years ago, a new thought hit me right between the eyes. Leggett was a veteran of the Civil War—did he by chance apply for a pension? I checked the online portal of the National Archives and Records Administration and found no record that he did. Then, a few weeks later, another idea woke me up. What if his wife, Alice, applied for a widow's pension? This would mean trying to prove, among other things, that Leggett served honorably, that she was still married to him—and that Joe Leggett was dead. In order to do that, Alice Leggett would have to provide a death certificate; if the death certificate used her husband's alias, she would presumably have to provide evidence that the alias and Joseph Leggett were the same person.

In 1899 Alice Leggett did apply for a military widow's pension. All I could find online, however, was an index card with file numbers and dates. Was there a paper file somewhere with all the applicable documents? After running down a few dead ends, I contacted archivist Adam Berenbak at NARA; several months later he told me that he had located a paper file. Inside it was a vein of pure gold. When

Alice Leggett struggled to prove to the satisfaction of the US Pension Office that Joe Leggett could be presumed dead based on his letters to her having stopped in 1882, 17 years earlier, she asked for help from a well-connected friend, Federal Treasury Department official and former Excelsiors ballplayer Colonel Frank Jones. Jones was also the man who had introduced her to her future husband. Jones turned to Charles D. Pennebaker, a well-connected Washington lawyer and future governor of Kentucky. Alice Leggett was retired and penniless, so it is safe to assume that it was Jones who paid him. The lawyer hired a private investigator to go to Leggett's last known location, Cheyenne, Wyoming, to try to pick up his trail.

In an earlier chapter, we told the story of how Joe Leggett got to Cheyenne, Wyoming and how he gambled away the cattle ranch that was supposed to be a new home for his wife and children. Leggett was then living under the alias Paul Mansfield. One of my hunches turned out to be half-right; Mansfield was the maiden name of Alice Leggett's mother. Today, Cheyenne is usually described as a quiet, peaceful place without much nightlife. But Leggett's Cheyenne was the booming no-rules frontier town with the nickname "Hell on Wheels." In the late 1870s Cheyenne had a population of 2,500. Living there were storied Wild West characters including Wild Bill Hickok, Buffalo Bill Cody, Bat Masterson, Doc Holliday and Calamity Jane. Paul Mansfield appears in the 1880 US Census, living in Cheyenne as a boarder in the home of a blacksmith named Sanders. This census asks heads of household to record if they are sick or disabled and why; next to Sanders's name the census taker scribbled the word "gunshot."

Alice and Joe Leggett's relatives claimed to have lost touch with him after he left Cheyenne around 1882, but Alice Leggett's investigator was able to trace his movements and uncover most of the story of Joe Leggett's 17 years in the West living as Paul Mansfield. His report paints a picture of Leggett that is typical of men who traded Victorian society for a rootless and solitary existence on the Western frontier. After letting his family down for the final time by gambling away his cattle ranch, Leggett went to Laramie County, Wyoming, and then Larimer County, Colorado, where he worked as a ranch hand for a cattleman named Charlie Andrews. Andrews bought farmland and eventually settled along the Cache la Poudre River near Fort Collins, Colorado, bringing Mansfield with him. The Colorado papers note Andrews's frequent visits to Denver in the 1880s. Between 1883 and 1892 there are dozens of reports of Paul Mansfield's presence in Denver. Mansfield was popular. In 1885, he was described as "a genial host...who is so well known and generally liked by all who have ever camped in the neighborhood." In 1884, Mansfield was appointed postmaster of Home; he later served as postmaster of nearby Chambers Lake and was elected to the county Democratic Committee and as a Justice of the Peace.

Paul Mansfield performed another service for Andrews. In the 1870s, 80s and 90s, the federal government encouraged economic development of the West by establishing land offices that sold parcels of land at a low price, with the requirement that the buyer meet development benchmarks such as grazing animals, sinking wells or building houses and barns. Speculators and ranchers often gamed the system by using straw buyers to purchase more land than they were entitled to; they also cheated by producing phony evidence that they were putting the land to use, including sworn false statements from witnesses. There were stories of owners putting barns on wheels and towing them from one property to another to fool government inspectors. A search of land office records turned up large tracts of land that were apparently acquired by Charlie Andrews in this way. Sometimes Andrews is the buyer and partners or employees are the witnesses; other times the same names change roles. Paul Mansfield can be found both as purchaser and witness. There is reason to doubt that he actually bought or worked any of the land; he continued to work as a ranch hand for Andrews throughout this period; there is no record of him developing or selling any of the land; and he died without a penny.

From the early 1880s to about 1892, Joe Leggett was living and working under the name Paul Mansfield in various places within a radius of less than one hundred miles of Denver. A well-known and popular figure, and the righthand man of a player in the cattle business, Mansfield spent a lot of time in Denver. In 1880 there were about thirty-five thousand people living in Denver; the population rose to about one hundred thousand by 1890. Did Joe Leggett ever blow his cover by bumping into a baseball fan from the East or someone who knew him from his previous life? He must have. Leggett was not the only man in Denver who had played for the pre-war Brooklyn Excelsiors. Benjamin Kimberley, a prominent Excelsior before the Civil War, moved to Denver in the early 1870s and never left. A Civil War hero, Kimberley became a popular politician, entrepreneur and cattle dealer. In the 1890s Kimberley was appointed to the office of "receiver;" this was the federal official who handled sales of public land. In 1888 Kimberley had an office in the Markham, Denver's finest hotel; he also regularly attended meetings at the Markham of the Grand Army of the Republic, a national organization of veterans of the Union Army. Kimberley was preceded in the Land Office by Louis Dugal, who was his next-door neighbor. With Paul Mansfield in and out of the Land Office on errands for Charlie Andrews, including during Kimberley's term as receiver, it is hard to imagine that the two did not cross paths. There is also the fact that Mansfield was a postmaster for much of the 1880s; postmasters were federal patronage appointments, not state, municipal or civil service jobs. Kimberley was the kind of well-connected figure who could easily arrange one as a sinecure for an old friend. This was, of course, one of the ways that the Excelsiors supported former players.

Denver was also home to another ex-Excelsior, Leggett's friend, teammate and former protégé Asa Brainard. Brainard and his brother Leonard were both living in the city in the middle and late 1880s. Until he died in 1888, Asa Brainard managed the billiards parlor of the Markham Hotel, which Kimberley frequented and where he had an office. Throughout the 1880s and 1890s, Kimberley's main business was cattle, but according to an 1887 Denver city directory, Leonard Brainard was employed as a clerk by J. B. Garland and Co., a railroad ticket brokerage that was co-owned by Ben Kimberley. The connections among Kimberley, the Brainard brothers and Mansfield/Leggett likely answer the question of how Henry Chadwick and other old baseball men in Brooklyn knew where Joe Leggett was in the 1880s.

In 1892, Paul Mansfield went to work for a gold ore assayer in Cripple Creek named J.C. Hames. Alice Leggett's private investigator tracked down Hames and showed him a photograph of Joe Leggett. Hames identified him as the man he knew as Mansfield. Hames describes Mansfield's mangled fingers, swollen joints and rheumatic shoulder—the price he paid for catching James Creighton in 1860. "I understood," Hames said, "he had been a baseball player."

In 1892 or 1893 Hames went to Galveston, Texas to pursue a real estate project and took Mansfield along. Mansfield lived with Hames until, as the Leggett family believed, he died in 1894. "He was buried in the cemetery in Dickinson," Hames said. "He died suddenly—it was 22 miles the nearest doctor, so we didn't know his cause of death. I think his grave was marked by a board slab. Mr. Mansfield told me he had a wife and children, a boy and a girl. He said his wife lived in Brooklyn, New York. He always spoke in the kindest way of his wife and children. He said she could not or would not live where he could and he had to live [in the] West on account of the climate, and she was not willing to live anywhere but the East; he said he [had] fixed her up in as good general shape as he could and that she could really get along better without him." The last part of that was certainly true.

JAMES CREIGHTON'S PLACE IN HISTORY

For most of the nineteenth century, James Creighton was famous as the pitcher *par excellence*. Albert Spalding's 1911 history of baseball, *America's National Game*, gives James Creighton his due for his greatness as a pitcher and for his leading role in the success of the Excelsiors and in making baseball our first national team sport. For more recent historians, however, Creighton's place in history has been reduced to being the first player to get away with being paid illegally, and one of the game's most successful on-field cheaters. Even well-meaning attempts to honor his legacy have gone wrong. If you go today to 307

Henry Street in Brooklyn, you will see that the building has a name: "The Creighton." Unfortunately, it is the wrong building. Because of a street renumbering in the 1870s, the 307 Henry Street where James Creighton died in 1862 is now number 461 Henry. Next door is 463 Henry Street, the building acquired by James Creighton, Sr. at the cost of his son's life. (Not far away is a rowhouse with a plaque identifying it as the birthplace of Winston Churchill's mother; this is also the wrong building.) In a better world, there would be an historical marker at the present 461 Henry Street informing passers-by that someone named James Creighton invented modern pitching in the backyard.

With the ever-increasing power and prestige of Major League Baseball in the twentieth and twenty-first centuries, there has been a natural tendency to emphasize the professional game to the exclusion of the Amateur Era and the rest of baseball's diverse ecosystem. This has come at a cost, however, in a poorer understanding of where baseball came from and why it developed the way it did. Early and pre-professional baseball are fascinating worlds that are worthy of our attention both for how they gave us modern baseball and in their own right.

There are several extant photographic prints that are purported to be the first baseball card. Trying to decide which has the better claim is a trip down yet another taxonomic rabbit hole. Baseball cards evolved from *cartes de visite*. These were originally personal calling cards; when photographic technology was sufficiently advanced in the mid-nineteenth century, they could be decorated with photographic images. Shortly after Creighton's death, photography studios and sporting goods dealers began mass-producing these and giving or selling them to fans and customers as keepsakes. Some, like the Atlantics' card on page 48 are team portraits. *Cartes de visite* featuring a single player became more common in the 1870s; they evolved into tobacco and then bubblegum trading cards. Experts disagree on the exact definition of a baseball card. Does it have to be sold with tobacco or gum? Does it have to be part of a set? Does it have to be attached to a particular kind of stock? As my brother the political reporter likes to say, I have nothing on that. But sometime between 1863 and 1868 the New

York City sporting goods company Peck and Snyder issued the first known commercially produced card with an image of one player. This player was no longer in baseball, but he was popular enough that his image was in great demand. When his card went on sale, Creighton had been dead for between one and six years.

The year 1968 may have been the nadir of James Creighton's historical reputation. Only a handful of serious histories of baseball had been published before that time. Few fans were interested in nineteenth-century baseball and sportswriters had lost interest after the last of the men who could tell them about it over a drink died of old age. The Society for American Baseball Research, or SABR, which inspired a revolution in historical research — and in other areas — was founded in 1971, but did not get much attention until the 1980s. In 1968, however, Robert Coover published his novel, *The Universal Baseball Association, Inc., J. Henry Waugh, proprietor*. Some say it is the best baseball novel ever written; others argue that it is a Christian allegory of man's (and Jesus's) relationship with God and that is not really about baseball at all. It is clear, however, that Coover knew his nineteenth-century baseball and that he had deep insight into the mind of a certain kind of baseball obsessive. The protagonist of Coover's novel is a solitary Brooklyn accountant named J. Henry Waugh (Yahweh, get it?) who creates a baseball simulation game based on probability and chance that is something like Strat-o-Matic baseball and other games in which fans act out their fantasies of being a manager, GM, owner, or a more elevated personage. In Waugh's game rolls of the dice move the action to charts of outcomes like base hits, outs and errors; rarer combinations of numbers lead to more unusual occurrences. Waugh invents players, gives them nicknames, personalities and skills, and plays out whole imaginary seasons, while keeping meticulous records and statistics. He gradually sinks into obsession and disconnection from reality. Waugh's most cherished creation is a physically and morally exemplary young pitcher modeled on James Creighton.

One day, however, the dice produce a particularly unlikely combination of numbers that causes his imaginary offspring to be killed.

Waugh spirals into grief and depression, at which point he meets a coworker in a bar. He begins to talk about the real James Creighton. "You know, Lou," he says, "when Jim Creighton died, the boys crowned his grave with a fantastic monument. It had crossed bats on it and a baseball cap and even a base and up on top a giant baseball. Or maybe it was the world. They probably no longer knew the difference." Waugh went on, "And you know what else they put on that monument, Lou…A scorebook!" For Coover's accountant baseball god, the game's significance derived ultimately from its numbers.

J. Henry Waugh's drinking companion had no idea who James Creighton was; the same was probably true of Coover's readers. In 1992, Creighton appears in an episode of *The Simpsons* TV show, in which Mr. Burns uses a baseball record book to pick a team to represent his nuclear power plant in a softball league. When he finds out that they are all dead, he replaces them with living MLB all-stars, but the original lineup included Hall of Famers like Honus Wagner and Three-finger Brown. Amazingly, Mr. Burns includes Creighton, but out of position in right field. Creighton was a pitcher and before that an infielder, but few *Simpsons* viewers would have known that.

The National Baseball Hall of Fame in Cooperstown is the place where baseball history is supposed to be preserved and remembered. As we have discussed, Creighton is absent from the Hall, and this has certainly diminished his standing in history. The Hall of Fame's relationship to the Amateur Era and early baseball history is a long and twisted tale, but its focus as an institution has always been, understandably, on the professional game. There are amateur greats with plaques, but all of them are there for other reasons, at least ostensibly. To pick one example, George Wright was elected to the Hall of Fame as an "executive/pioneer," not as the greatest all-around shortstop of his time. There have been efforts to put James Creighton into the Hall of Fame. In 2019 SABR's Nineteenth Century Committee voted Creighton its annual "Overlooked 19th-century Baseball Legend" award. The purpose of this award is to raise public awareness of deserving but neglected players. Sometimes it works; Deacon White won in 2010 and made it into the Hall three years later. James Creighton rates a single mention in Bill James's 1995 book on the Hall of Fame. Addressing MLB's eminent official historian, James writes, "John Thorn, say a word for yourself. We'll never get Jim Creighton in the Hall of Fame, but your opinion should carry as much weight as anybody else's."

Ironically, James Creighton was one of the first names that popped up when the Baseball Hall of Fame was first discussed in the mid-1930s. Alexander Cleland, the idea man behind the Hall, wrote a letter in 1935 proposing kicking off the project with an exhibition of fifty baseball immortals. "The fifty immortals," he wrote, "would, of course, be headed by Abner Doubleday... then it would be an open field for the George and Harry Wrights, A. G. Spalding, Dan McBride [sic], Creighton, Leggett, down the line through Anson, Brouthers, Keeler, Wagner, Hornsby, Lajoie, Cobb, Mathewson, Walsh to Babe Ruth."

Bill James's book discusses the arbitrary and ahistorical way that both the Hall of Fame and generations of sportswriters have shaped our views of baseball's past. There are many infamous cases of deserving players forgotten and of mediocrities honored or given credit for the achievements of others. Cummings and the curveball is a case in point. At the close of the nineteenth century, when people began to look back and ask who threw the first curveball, Arthur Cummings was a popular and widely known baseball man. He told a compelling story that journalists could use. Most importantly, he was around.

There were baseball players with direct, firsthand knowledge that James Creighton had thrown a curve far earlier than Cummings — men like Joe Leggett, Asa Brainard and Creighton himself. Why didn't they speak up? We already know the answer to that question. Joe Leggett disappeared in 1877. Asa Brainard died in Colorado in 1888. Creighton himself died in 1862. One reason that James Creighton has been forgotten for so long is that there has been no one to speak for him.

SOURCES & BILBLIOGRAPHY

IMPORTANT WORKS ON EARLY BASEBALL HISTORY

Block, David. *Baseball Before We Knew It: A Search for the Roots of the Game*: University of Nebraska Press, 2005. This is a groundbreaking work on the origins and history of the *game* of baseball, that is, baseball before it became a *sport* in the mid-nineteenth-century New York City and Brooklyn metropolitan area.

Chadwick, Henry. *The Game of Base Ball.* Reprint Edition: Camden House, 1983. Part history and part instructional, this is a reprint of the first baseball book, originally published in 1868. Nineteenth-century baseball's most important journalist, Chadwick served on baseball's rules committee, influenced the evolution and spread of the sport, and adapted or invented the box score and most of its basic statistics.

Gilbert, Thomas W. *How Baseball Happened: Outrageous Lies Exposed! The True Story Revealed*: Godine, 2020. In his introduction to this book, MLB Official Historian John Thorn writes, "Robert Henderson and David Block addressed the origins of bat-and-ball games (the *where* and *when*) around the world. My own *Baseball in the Garden of Eden* moved from Europe and Africa to America and addressed the *what*, i.e., the facts surrounding the game's beginnings rather than what self-anointed fathers of the game wished us to believe. Gilbert addresses how baseball happened and, delightfully, its anagram of *who*."

Henderson, Robert. *Bat, Ball and Bishop: The Origin of Ball Games*: Rockport Press, 1947. The original (and still effective) antidote to the Doubleday and other false baseball origin tales.

Jensen, Don, Editor. *BASE BALL, New Research on the Early Game,* Volumes 10,11 and 12: McFarland & Company, 2018–2021

Morris, Peter et al., Editors. *Baseball Founders*: McFarland & Company, 2013.

Morris, Peter et al., Editors. *Baseball Pioneers, 1850–1870*: McFarland & Company, 2012.

Both of the above books are invaluable references containing an amazing amount of new biographical information on thousands of formerly anonymous Amateur Era baseball men.

Orem, Preston D. *Baseball (1845–1881) From the Newspaper Accounts.* Altadena: Published by the Author, 1961. A quirky selection of newspaper clippings about nineteenth-century baseball, this book was more valuable in the days before newspaper digitization, but it still provides useful information and context for the sport of baseball's early decades.

Peverelly, Charles. *The Book of American Pastimes, Containing a History of the Principal Base Ball, Cricket, Rowing, and Yachting Clubs of the United States.* New York: Published by the Author, 1866. One chapter of this book constitutes the first serious attempt at a history of the important early baseball clubs. It is uneven because the author sent queries to those of the clubs that were active around 1865 and uncritically included whatever they sent him about their records and history.

Seymour, Harold, Dorothy Seymour Mills. *Baseball: The Early Years*: Oxford University Press, 1960. A lot of new ground has been broken in early baseball history since 1960, but all things considered this large and scholarly work, volume one of a three-volume history of baseball, has aged well.

Spalding, Albert G. *Baseball: America's National Game 1839–1915*: American Sports, 1911. Spalding has a bad name because of his role in creating the Abner Doubleday lie in 1907, but he made baseball's first attempt at a serious history. The author was an eyewitness, contemporary and key figure in baseball for much of the sport's first half-century. He can be sloppy, pompous — and right.

Thorn, John. *Baseball in the Garden of Eden: The Secret History of the Early Game*: Simon and Schuster, 2011. An authoritative and elegantly written work on pre-professional baseball from the godfather of baseball history.

Thorn, John, Editor. *BASE BALL, New Research on the Early Game*, Volumes 1–9: McFarland & Company, 2007–2017

Wright, Marshall D. *The National Association of Base Ball Players, 1857–1870*: McFarland & Company, 2000. The most reliable baseball reference for the chaotic Amateur Era.

OTHER WORKS

Adelman, Melvin L. *A Sporting Time: New York City and the Rise of Modern Athletics, 1820–1870*: University of Illinois Press, 1990.

Coover, Robert. *The Universal Baseball Association Inc. J. Henry Waugh Prop*: Rupert Hart-Davis, 1970. A wildly original and eccentric novel that takes an indirect route into the soul of fandom.

Dreifort, John E. *Baseball History from Outside the Lines*: University of Nebraska Press, 2001.

Gilbert, Thomas W. *Playing First: Early Baseball Lives at Brooklyn's Green-Wood Cemetery*: Green-Wood Cemetery, 2015. This book asks and attempts to answer the question: why are hundreds of important baseball pioneers buried in the same cemetery?

Goldstein, Warren. *Playing For Keeps: A History of Early Baseball*: Cornell University Press, 1989.

Hershberger, Richard. *Strike Four: The Evolution of Baseball*: Rowman and Littlefield, 2019. This book needs a new subtitle—it is narrowly focused on the evolution of the rules, not the sport in a broad sense—but it is full of useful information.

James, Bill. *Whatever Happened to the Hall of Fame?*: Simon and Schuster, 1994. An illuminating book on a topic that is not entirely worthy of its author.

Lovett, James D'Wolf. *Old Boston Boys and the Games They Played.* Boston: Privately Printed, 1906.

Melville, Tom. *The Tented Field: A History of Cricket in America*: Bowling Green University Popular Press, 1998.

Melville, Tom. *This Too Was America: Philadelphia's Era of Cricket.*: McFarland, 2023.

Rucker, Mark. *Base Ball Cartes: The First Baseball Cards*: Haymaker Books, 1988.

Ryczek, William J. *Baseball's First Inning: A History of the National Pastime Through the Civil War*: McFarland, 2009.

Thorn, John and Holway, John. *The Pitcher*: Prentice Hall, 1987

Ellard, Harry. *Base Ball in Cincinnati: A History.* Cincinnati: Subscription Edition, 1907.

NEWSPAPERS, PERIODICALS AND DATABASES

The best sources for nineteenth-century baseball history are the national sports weeklies, which were published in New York City, along with the New York City and Brooklyn daily papers. Some of these are digitized; others are available on microfilm or otherwise in libraries and archives.

DIGITIZED AND AVAILABLE ONLINE (SOME SUBSCRIPTION ONLY):

The New York Clipper: Illinois Digital Newspaper Collections https://idnc.library.illinois.edu

Newspapers.com: Contains editions of the Brooklyn *Daily Eagle* and many other Brooklyn and New York City papers.

Genealogy.com: Contains the *New York Times* and many other Brooklyn and New York City papers.

Hudson River Valley Heritage https://news.hrvh.org

California Digital Newspaper Collection https://cdnc.ucr.edu/cgi-bin/cdnc

http://www.fultonhistory.com/Fulton.html

http://nyshistoricnewspapers.org/

The Sporting Life Magazine: https://digital.la84.org/digital/collection/p17103coll17/search

AVAILABLE FROM THE LIBRARY OF CONGRESS AND OTHER LIBRARIES:

The Spirit of the Times 1837–1861
Wilkes' Spirit of the Times 1859–1868
The New England Base Ballist 1868
The Sunday Mercury 1839–1897
The National Chronicle 1869–1870
The New York Atlas 1855–1861
The Philadelphia Sunday Mercury
The Philadelphia City Item
The Ball Player's Chronicle

Mears Baseball Scrapbooks 1853–1869
https://cplorg.contentdm.oclc.org/digital/collection/p4014coll27/id/346/

NON-JOURNALISTIC SOURCES:

NARA
https://www.archives.gov/

National Park Service Soliders and Sailors Civil War Database
https://www.nps.gov/civilwar/soldiers-and-sailors-database.htm

Hathi Trust Digital Library
https://www.hathitrust.org/

Google Books
https://books.google.com/

Jstor
https://www.jstor.org/

Stevens Digital Collections
https://librarycollections.stevens.edu/

John Thorn's OurGame Blog
https://ourgame.mlblogs.com/

Protoball
https://protoball.org/Chronologies

New York Genealogical and Biographical Society
https://www.newyorkfamilyhistory.org/

Family Search
https://www.familysearch.org/

Ancestry.com
https://www.ancestry.com/

New York Historical Society
https://www.nyhistory.org/

New York Public Library
https://www.nypl.org/

Library of Congress
https://www.loc.gov/

University of Michigan Digital Collections
https://quod.lib.umich.edu/lib/colllist/

American Antiquarian Society
https://www.americanantiquarian.org/

Find a Grave
https://www.findagrave.com/

Green-Wood
https://www.green-wood.com/

National Baseball Hall of Fame
https://baseballhall.org/the-museum/library-research

Center for Brooklyn History
http://www.bklynlibrary.org/center-for-brooklyn-history

SABR
https://sabr.org/

ACKNOWLEDGMENTS

THIS IS A HARD PART of the book to write, because I have so many people to thank. No one accomplishes much of anything by themselves. History is even more collaborative than most endeavors.

I spent years researching and pondering the brief life of James Creighton, but this, his first biography, owes a great debt to the many baseball researchers, scholars and eccentrics who have contributed so much to Our Thing — early baseball history.

Special thanks to the learned John Thorn, my good friend, for your inspiring example, sage advice and delightful conversation over the years.

Thank you, Peter Mancuso, Bob Bailey, the late, greatly missed Larry McCray, Jon Popovich, David Block, Robert Tholkes, Richard Hershberger, Bill Ryczek, Priscilla Astifan, Maury Bouchard, Paul Langendorfer, Don Jensen, Bill Humber and my other friends and colleagues at the Society for American Baseball Research and SABR's all-star Nineteenth-Century Committee. It takes each of us pulling our oar to move the ship forward. The ship is moving. Every year, we learn more about baseball's beginnings.

To Tom Shieber of the National Baseball Hall of Fame; I could not have come even this close to harpooning this particular white whale without your astounding generosity: thank you.

Thank you, Sal Guerriero, for helping me understand James Creighton's pitching, and for driving all the way from Delaware to show me. Thanks to Adam Berenbak at NARA and to my old friend, Tony Freeman, whose enthusiasm for this project kept me going. Thanks also, Tony, for all the time you spent looking in Texas for the man formerly known as Joe Leggett.

Thank you, David Allender and everyone at Godine, my author's dream of a publisher, for your support and expertise, and for putting my name on two of your beautiful books. I am grateful to David Godine, a national treasure, for his advice and counsel. Thank you, Jerry Kelly, for your work, your friendship and your support.

Neither I nor this book would be here without the love and affection of my wife, Lisa Gilbert, who must be looking forward to many golden years of not having to talk about how James Creighton gripped his curveball. Thank you to my brother Craig and the rest of my family: my children Wesley and Susannah, my son-in-law Akif, daughter-in-law Iida; and my beautiful grandchildren Eliza, Wayne and Oliver. I am prouder of you all than I could be of any book.

INDEX